POLISHED
But not
PERFECT

D1613185

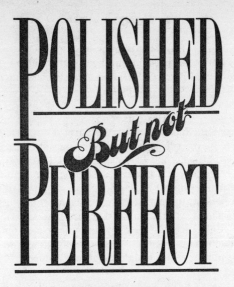

POLISHED But not PERFECT

Toos Rosies

Preface by Elisabeth Elliot

OM Publishing
Bromley, Kent

© Toos Rosies 1990

First English edition published 1990
Translated and revised from the original Dutch titles
Je Bent Goud Waard (1987) and *Medewerkers Gezocht*
(1988)

Scripture quotations are taken from the HOLY BIBLE,
NEW INTERNATIONAL VERSION, © 1973, 1978, 1984
by International Bible Society and published in Britain by
Hodder & Stoughton Ltd.

British Library Cataloguing in Publication Data

Rosies, Toos
  Polished but not perfect.
  1. Christian theology
  I. Title
  230

ISBN 1-85078-069-2

OM Publishing is an imprint of Send The Light
(Operation Mobilisation),
PO Box 48, Bromley, Kent, England, BR1 3JH

Production and Printing in England by
Nuprint Ltd, Station Road, Harpenden, Herts, AL5 4SE.

Contents

Preface

Polished but Not Perfect, the testimony of a young Dutch woman who offered to God all that she has and is, has the ring of reality as she allows us glimpses into her heart and her home and her family life. Applying lessons from the lives of women in the Bible, she plainly shows the meaning of trust and obedience, and does not omit the cost for those who intend to follow the one who bore a cross.

Elisabeth Elliot

Introduction

POLISHED BUT NOT PERFECT

'Is something wrong with my baby?'

I had just given birth to my second son and lay back on the delivery table in exhaustion. His first cry was loud and clear. With my eyes closed I waited happily for the moment they would show me the baby. After several minutes I realised that something unusual was going on. Doctors and nurses stood whispering around the baby and then disappeared with the child to another room. A minute later the doctor called my husband, Kees, away from me, while a midwife tried to divert my attention. When Kees came back to my side, I was sure by the look on his face that something was seriously wrong.

He told me that the baby had only one eye and that they were not sure about some other things either. They had taken him away for further examination.

The next few hours were very hard. Nobody could tell for certain to what extent he would be handicapped. The left eye and the eye nerve were totally missing. There was not even an eye socket. Something had gone wrong in the early months of pregnancy and it was not clear if there would be further physical or mental problems.

God's grace and comfort were overwhelming in those

first days of struggle and sadness. With God's help we were able to accept the child the way he was.

Ophthalmologists and paediatricians observed him carefully in his development. Slowly but surely it became obvious that, apart from his eye, he was healthy and normal.

In order to create an eye socket for an artificial eye, he needed a lot of medical treatment. During the first three years of his life, we spent most Mondays in the university hospital. It was a long, painstaking, slow and often nerve-racking process; a process in which a physical imperfection was slowly being transformed into what it should have been in the first place.

The effect of this long and slow process has been amazing. Today my son is a good-looking twenty-one-year-old, who is studying medicine at the University of Louvain in Belgium, where we live. Of course he has no sight in his left eye, since it is made of glass. But the patient perseverance of his ophthalmologist during his early childhood has resulted in the forming of a face which looks so normal that even his best friends do not easily notice the problem.

This slow process of change through much perseverance and painstaking effort is a good picture of the change God wants to carry out in our lives, after we have been born into his family. When we come to him, we come with a sinful nature, with bad habits and with wounds on our souls. He invites us to come to him the way we are. The Bible says that he loves those who come to him with the broken pieces of their lives. 'He will not break the bruised reed, nor quench the dimly burning flame. He will encourage the faint-hearted, those tempted to despair' (Isaiah 42:3). But that is not the end of the story. When we come to him, he wants to straighten out our deformed lives, he wants to make us perfect, in the image of his Son. But this is a long and slow process. It will take a lifetime.

I began my life-changing process about thirty years ago, when I surrendered my life to Christ at the age of sixteen, in a camp in the Netherlands, my home country. Many things had to change and God used the Bible and his Spirit, and also circumstances and people, to bring about some of these changes. Twenty-five years of marriage certainly had some polishing effects on Kees and me! Bringing up our two sons, Jonathan and Henno, and our two Korean-born adopted daughters, Marlies and Karin, also played its part in the process. Facing daily challenges in our many years of missionary involvement forced me time and time again to turn to God for help in changing those things in my life which were still so far from perfect.

As the children have grown up, I have been able to spend more time in a ministry of speaking, writing and counselling, mainly with women. I have discovered that many women are facing the same problems that I have struggled with.

My desire for this book is that you may grasp the picture God has in mind for your life. It is a great, exciting and encouraging picture. The crucial thing is, however, that he wants and needs our co-operation in order to accomplish the changes that will have to come in the practical aspects of our daily lives. Even more change will have to take place in our inner lives, dealing with the characteristics and weaknesses that prevent us becoming more like Jesus. It is my prayer, therefore, that you, through this book, might be encouraged to be 'Polished but not Perfect' and to take your rightful place in the body of Christ.

1

Superwoman!

The words of Proverbs 31 continue to amaze and inspire me. The picture painted for us in these verses is of an exceptional woman. She is the kind of woman I admire and would love to be—versatile, modern, enterprising, strong, wise and possessing a host of other qualities and characteristics for which any godly woman should strive. It's difficult to imagine that these verses were written so many hundreds of years ago, and yet remain so relevant today. It greatly encourages me that God inspired this beautiful passage and chose it to be put in his Word, specifically to inspire women and serve as an example for many who would live in later ages.

> A wife of noble character who can find?
>   She is worth far more than rubies.
> Her husband has full confidence in her,
>   and lacks nothing of value.
> She brings him good, not harm,
>   all the days of her life.
> She selects wool and flax
>   and works with eager hands.
> She is like the merchant ships,
>   bringing her food from afar.
> She gets up while it is still dark;
>   she provides food for her family

   and portions for her servant girls.
She considers a field and buys it;
   out of her earnings she plants a vineyard.
She sets about her work vigorously;
   her arms are strong for her tasks.
She sees that her trading is profitable,
   and her lamp does not go out at night.
In her hand she holds the distaff
   and grasps the spindle with her fingers.
She opens her arms to the poor
   and extends her hands to the needy.
When it snows, she has no fear for her household;
   for all of them are clothed in scarlet.
She makes coverings for her bed;
   she is clothed in fine linen and purple.
Her husband is respected at the city gate,
   where he takes his seat among the elders of the land.
She makes linen garments and sells them,
   and supplies the merchants with sashes.
She is clothed with strength and dignity;
   she can laugh at the days to come.
She speaks with wisdom,
   and faithful instruction is on her tongue.
She watches over the affairs of her household,
   and does not eat the bread of idleness.
Her children arise and call her blessed;
   her husband also, and he praises her:
Many women do noble things,
   but you surpass them all.
Charm is deceptive, and beauty is fleeting;
   but a woman who fears the Lord is to be praised.
Give her the reward she has earned,
   and let her works bring her praise at the city gate.
(Proverbs 31:10–31)

A PRICELESS GEM

To some of us the word 'noble' conjures up a picture of long dresses, a hair-style from the year zero and a 'stiff upper lip' attitude. But it actually has a much more positive meaning. It simply means a good woman, beautiful person or as one of our friends always says of his wife; 'She's the best.'

The passage tells us that such a person is not easily found. It's going to mean hard work for us to even get close to being such a woman. 'She is worth far more than rubies.' Such a woman is extremely precious. Reading through this chapter, you realise that such a capable, spiritual, good and zealous wife, as the centre of a family, indeed is priceless! You do not become such a woman in a couple of days. It takes a lot of time, concerted effort, self-discipline and self-denial. When you are in the process of growing and developing in this direction, it's not easy keeping the glorious picture in your mind's eye. Don't those of us who are wives and mothers often exclaim out of pure irritation and frustration; 'I'm not a centipede!' or 'I've only got one pair of hands!' because the task we have to do by far exceeds our capacity and strength. It is good to regularly reflect on the words; 'she is worth far more than rubies' and just allow God himself to encourage us. So take courage and press on, because what you're becoming is a priceless gem.

In his book about women and their emotional lives (*Man to Man About Women*) James Dobson writes that the biggest problem that many women face is the deeprooted feeling of inferiority. Housewives are particularly prone to this feeling of being without worth, as our society regards them as being without an occupation. It's a must for every Christian woman to read Proverbs 31 regularly, or preferably memorise it, so that even the

slightest feeling of inferiority can immediately be rooted
out. The woman we're striving to be is versatile,
vivacious, capable and efficient, so there is absolutely no
room left for feelings of inferiority. We need to come to
the realisation that we are indeed priceless and more
precious than gold, yet not in our own strength, but in
God's.

What then are the qualities which make the Proverbs
31 woman special? The key is in verse 30; '...but a
woman who fears the Lord is to be praised.' Before we
do anything or become anything for the Lord, our lives
have to be dedicated to him. I was only seventeen when,
at a tent-meeting at our chilly campsite in the spacious
flat countryside of the Netherlands during the rainy summer of 1959, I really dedicated my life to God's service.
Looking back, I realise how young I was and how little I
knew about life. Nevertheless, my decision was real and
became the turning point in my life, at the time when
young people are expected to make crucial decisions
regarding their future. The wonderful thing about your
dedication to God is that when you take your first hesi-
tant steps in his direction and offer him your small,
insignificant life, you soon discover that he receives you
with open arms, embraces you and showers you with
gifts, as he changes your life. Just as the prodigal son had
no idea what would happen to him when he decided, in
his utter misery, to return to his father, so we have no
idea what God will do with our lives when we arrive on
his doorstep.

I remember very well how pleasantly surprised I was
when I began to see what God was doing in my life. A
deep love for him and a hunger for his Word was born in
my heart, closely followed by a genuine love for my
fellow Christians as new brothers and sisters. Until then,
I had not been able to understand the Bible. However,
after God's Spirit came to dwell in my heart, the reading

of his Word became a fascinating treasure hunt. His work with its worldwide perspectives became my key interest and I had a direction into which I could channel all my enthusiasm. Never again did I doubt what to do with my life. This was a cause to live for!

Now, many years later, I still hold fast to that same conviction. I know much more now compared to what I knew then. I have learned some hard lessons and I have lost some of my illusions. But more than ever, I am convinced that the Lord's cause is the best one to live for.

The woman of Proverbs 31 had learnt the secret of serving God. As we read on through the passage, most of us will agree that in our own nature we do not possess most of the virtues of this wonderful woman. But we can acquire them! This woman feared the Lord. She had given her life to him, and, after that original decision and surrender, she had carefully sustained her fellowship with him. Such a personal spiritual life does not come by doing nothing. It will only grow by personal devotion and by continually reflecting on who God is. We will grow if we discipline ourselves to open the Bible daily and to study God's Word, if we learn to pray and get used to spending time with God, so that he can begin to form these characteristics in our lives, through his Holy Spirit. These characteristics are the same as the fruit of the Spirit, which Paul describes in Galatians 5:22:

> But the fruit of the Spirit is love, joy, peace, patience, kindness, goodness, faithfulness, gentleness and self-control.

Reading about all the activities of the woman of Proverbs 31, you wonder how her family reacted to such a busy and hard-working mother and wife. Did they not suffer because of all her activities? At the end of the chapter, we read how positively her family felt. In verse

28 we see that 'her children arise and call her blessed'. That is wonderful! They are convinced that they have a wonderful mum! They love and admire her, and it's no hassle for them to do extra jobs around the house to help her out. 'Her husband also, and he praises her.' Dad and the boys completely agree that not many women can be compared with their mother and wife. The girls in the family do not grow up with inferiority complexes about being a woman. No, they have an inspiring example and, like their mum, they are positive and cheerful about the days when they themselves will be grown up and will lead this same fulfilling life.

Throughout the years I have come to know many families of different nationalities and backgrounds, and I have observed the following; the most important characteristic of a Christian wife and mother towards her family is her attitude towards life. A mother and wife who loves the Lord, who lives with him, and who faces life in a positive and enthusiastic way can expect positive fruit in her family as well. The last verse of this chapter says, 'Give her the reward she has earned.' We will reap what we have sown. If we have sown a positive attitude towards life and lots of enthusiasm for God and his purpose, we can certainly hope to see this develop in our children.

There is, of course, no guarantee that our children will follow in our footsteps. John White states this strongly in his book *Parents in Pain*. Children make their own choices in life, and they are ultimately responsible to God for the decisions they make. But a happy and motivated mother is probably the most positive influence in a child's life. What and how much you're involved in outside the home is not the determining factor. It's common for children whose parents have eagerly served the Lord to have a positive attitude towards life and God,

even though they had to sometimes 'step in' when Mum
and Dad were not around.

On the other hand, when the father is very dedicated
to the Lord's work, but the mother stays out of it, her
attitude is very important. An attitude of self-pity, complaining and bitterness towards that which her husband
is doing soon becomes obvious also in the children,
because after all she spends most of her time with them.
She largely influences them in their attitudes towards life
and towards God. If her attitude is negative and bitter, it
will bear its bad fruit in her children.

In the woman of Proverbs 31 we encounter an attitude
to life which radiates joy, strength, enthusiasm and a
positive devotion to all life's events. She will reap the
fruit of that. 'Give her the reward she has earned, and let
her works bring her praise at the city gate.'

2

Deciding Your Priorities

A friend of mine, Joni, told me about the first time she went out to Africa to work with her husband as a missionary. Her husband had to go overland, leading a party of young people with vehicles and other equipment across Europe, the Mediterranean and the seemingly endless Sahara Desert, on a difficult and possibly dangerous journey. Joni, meanwhile, had to cope with taking their two babies on her first flight to Africa. Her husband's party had left several weeks before, and she expected him to be waiting for her at the airport. When her aeroplane landed on the dusty runway, Joni's eager eyes searched with apprehension for the familiar face of her husband. However, there was no one there to welcome her and the children. His journey had taken longer than expected. The overland party only arrived a few days later. Somehow, Joni survived.

When I expressed my admiration for her courage, Joni answered, 'Toos, had it not been for the Lord Jesus, I could never have done it.' Isn't this the essence of our dedication! 'If it was not for the Lord Jesus...'! That's the difference; it was for the Lord Jesus, therefore she did it, and they will do it again and again. It was not easy when they went the first time, nor more recently when they went for the third time. With temperatures rising to

120°F, and a shortage of many essentials, it never will be easy. Yet they go—young people, families, mothers with new-born babies. They go, because of the Lord Jesus.

Are they extra-special women, much braver than the rest of us mere mortal beings? I don't think so! They are women like you and me, with their good characteristics, their weaknesses and their concern for their children. They also lie awake at night when these kinds of decisions have to be made. They are just as scared as everybody else but they decide to go anyway, because their lives are founded on a personal commitment to Christ.

Personal dedication

Most of us know that salvation is a personal matter, but how many of us realise that obedience and the decision to dedicate our life to God is just as personal? How often do we hide behind our husbands or circumstances? We tell ourselves that we cannot and should not make any personal decisions. Instead we are to be 'submissive' and that settles it for a 'good Christian housewife'.

However, this seemingly positive attitude is really nothing more than an escape-route. How can a woman be submissive in the biblical sense, if this submission is not founded on a personal dedication to Christ? What would be your reaction if your fiancé or husband decided to give up his well-paid job to become a missionary? What would be left of your faith if your husband suddenly died? Nothing on this earth is permanent, not even a good Christian marriage. Your personal relationship to God is all that will remain when it comes to exchanging time for eternity.

I am genuinely shocked and upset when I notice the lack of motivation in the lives of many girls and women.

Most people no longer have a goal to work towards in life. So instead of being able to see what they have achieved day by day, they start their lives over again every week, and spend yet another chunk of their time totally unrelated to their life-time goals.

If you are on your own for a lot of the time, for example as a housewife, you will need a good deal of self-discipline and definite goals. The temptation could otherwise prove too strong to go back to bed for a few hours, sit reading the paper for a seemingly endless amount of time, or to indulge in gossip with your next-door neighbour. Before you know it, another day has passed and nothing has been achieved.

Or what if you are about to choose a job or profession? Do you know what your goals in life are? Is it proper for a Christian to choose a particular profession simply because 'you should study something'? What motivates you to accept a boring, poorly-paid job? Could it be that secretly you're only waiting to be 'discovered' or swept off your feet by some handsome prince? While you're waiting for this fairy tale to happen, some of life's most precious years and moments will pass you by, years in which you could have learned and accomplished so much. The reality that so many young people play around with important months and years of their lives is largely due to a basic lack of motivation and vision.

Women in the New Testament

God's Word is very clear and it applies to us women just as much as to the men. In Galatians 3:28 Paul states that there is no difference between male and female in being accepted. This is one of the great virtues of the Christian faith, in comparison to other world religions. God does not consider us women to be 'second-class' citizens. God gave women a place of honour in his Word.

It is wonderful to discover the revolutionary way in which the Lord Jesus himself acknowledged this. Reading through the Gospels we see that Jesus taught some of his deepest spiritual truths to women. Think of the Samaritan woman at the well in John 4. In those days, it was certainly not the norm for rabbis to share their knowledge with women. So, when the disciples returned from their shopping, they were rather surprised to find Jesus talking to a woman. But this didn't deter Jesus, he continued talking to her about streams of living water welling up to eternal life. It is clear from this account that the woman was well able to appreciate Jesus' words. She herself believed and many Samaritans from that city came to believe in him as a result of her testimony (John 4:39).

Further on in the Gospel of John, we see how Jesus teaches important spiritual matters to Martha and Mary. For example, in chapter 11 he tells them, ' "I am the resurrection and the life. He who believes in me will live, even though he dies; and whoever lives and believes in me will never die. Do you believe this?" "Yes, Lord," [Martha] told him, "I believe that you are the Christ, the Son of God, who was to come into the world" ' (John 11:25–27). How far-reaching are his words to these women and how full of faith and understanding of his nature is Martha's answer!

Then at the resurrection, to our amazement and joy, we see that the Lord Jesus appears first to a woman (John 20). Mary Magdalene becomes the very first witness of Jesus' return from the dead and has the privilege of proclaiming the good news to the men. The strange thing is that when Paul, many years later, gives a list of the people to whom Jesus appeared after his resurrection, he does not even mention Mary. The witness of a woman had no value for the Jews. But the Lord breaks through these traditions and reveals himself first to Mary.

In the Book of Acts we see how women have played an important role in the first churches and in the spreading of the gospel. The first person in Europe who became a Christian and was baptised was a woman, Lydia, the seller of purple cloth. The Macedonian man of Paul's dream turned out to be a woman in real life. After her conversion she invited Paul and his team to use her home as a base from which the work could be continued. When we then read the names of the people in Romans 16 to whom Paul sends his greetings, it includes the names of many women in Europe who followed in Lydia's footsteps. Paul goes on to commend others to them; 'Phoebe, a servant of the church in Cenchreae . . . for she has been a great help to many people, including me. Greet Priscilla and Aquilla, my fellow-workers in Christ Jesus. They risked their lives for me . . . Greet Mary, who worked very hard for you'—and lots of other women, like Tryphena and Tryphosa, Persis, the mother of Rufus, Julia and the sister of Nereus. All of them women, commended for their hard work in God's kingdom.

As we have seen, the Bible speaks very clearly of the fact that there is no distinction between men and women concerning salvation and the grace we have received in Christ. Also in Acts 2 and Joel 2, it is evident that the Holy Spirit is given to women in the same way as to men. We read in Acts 2:17,18 about both sons and daughters who shall prophesy and about men and women servants upon whom God shall pour out his Spirit. No, there is no room or reason to doubt in this matter!

In 1 Corinthians 12 we read about the gifts of the Spirit. We are told in this chapter that we all, men and women, have been baptised by the Spirit into one body and that the Spirit gives gifts to each one in the body, as he wills! (1 Corinthians 12:12–27). Since the Bible is so clear as to all of these wonderful privileges which we women have received, just as much as the men, why then shouldn't the same devotion and dedication be asked of us?

Our definite call to this dedication is mentioned in the Bible as frequently as the description of our privileges. Paul says 'Do your best to present yourself to God as one approved, a workman who does not need to be ashamed' (2 Timothy 2:15). He also appeals to us 'to offer [our] bodies as living sacrifices to God' (Romans 12:1) and to 'be very careful...how [we] live—not as unwise but as wise, making the most of every opportunity' (Ephesians 5:15,16). He challenges us: 'Do you not know that in a race all the runners run, but only one gets the prize? Run in such a way as to get the prize' (1 Corinthians 9:24). The call is clear: do your best, pay careful attention to what you do with your life and give your all to attain that prize! In 1 Corinthians 9 Paul continues to tell us that athletes give all their strength and time to win a perishable prize and how true this is as we stop to consider how frequently most world records change these days! But our race is based on eternal values.

So many of us think that we have an option! We can freely choose to live for God, or to go our own way. But as I read the Bible, I realise that the second option has very serious consequences. Looking closer at Paul's example of the athlete, I cannot help but notice that he in no way treated this matter lightly. At the end of 1 Corinthians 9 he said: 'I do not run like a man running aimlessly; I do not fight like a man beating the air. No, I beat my body and make it my slave so that after I have preached to others, I myself will not be disqualified for the prize.' These words show us that the call to dedication is to be taken seriously.

The place of the family

What is the place of the family in all this? Should not our primary dedication as wives and mothers be to our own families?

It is certainly true that the family is under severe attack today. Different forms of 'living together' are generally accepted in society. People with high ideals about marriage very quickly discover that such a partnership does not survive only on love and fresh air, and often their marriage ends in divorce or separation. So children are forced to grow up robbed of one parent. It is fortunate that God gave children an enormous amount of flexibility and ability to adjust. Of the many children who have to cope with serious problems in their early years, quite a few seem to manage, but the lives of so many others are seriously affected.

It is no wonder then that Christians have come out strongly in defence of the family unit. Books have been written, Bible studies have been taught, conferences have been organised and we have become very 'family-conscious'. This has motivated us afresh, we now understand background influences a lot better, we have learned to solve problems and we have received weapons for ourselves and for our children to defend our precious families against the anti-family influences that threaten to inundate us all.

But sometimes I get the feeling that our families have become the ultimate goal of our lives, and that is not actually what we find in the Bible. Although the family is the basic structure of our society, according to the Bible, the ultimate object of our lives is higher. To love God, to live for his glory, to make his name known, to make disciples of all the nations; these are just some of the goals which are clear in the Bible.

Sometimes, when these ultimate goals collide with family life, the Lord even tells us that our ideas of the ideal family will have to be sacrificed for the other and higher aim. Luke 14:26 is a difficult but clear verse. Jesus says; 'If anyone comes to me and does not hate his father and mother, his wife and children, his brothers and sisters—yes, even his own life—he cannot be my disciple.' The verb 'hate' here does not mean an absence of love, but a willingness to give up, and to put God first. It would communicate clearly the fact that in case of conflict, God's business is more important than family life.

I cannot help but think about our brothers and sisters who live in countries where there has been little freedom of religion. If they had remained silent and followed the instructions of their governments, they would have been allowed to enjoy their fine families in peace. We all know however that they did not remain silent and that many of the fathers and some of the mothers spent most of those precious family years in prison or labour camps, while their children were being educated in atheistic children's homes. Christians in these countries came to the conclusion that family life is not the ultimate goal we live for and they have paid a high price for putting this conviction into practice.

We have read and studied so much about family life these days; about psychology, and family planning, and mothers working outside the home, the kind of education our children should get and how we can discipline them, that we now think that we know all the answers and we even wonder if someone with different ideas to ours could be a good Christian.

But in fact the Bible only gives us very few examples of 'good' families in our concept of that word. The Old Testament and even the New Testament show us families of the eastern way of life, in which several generations and branches of the same large family live together. In the Old Testament we even find many families where there are several wives with one husband. It is consoling to see that some very wonderful people have come out of far from ideal family situations!

Think of Joseph! His father had two wives and two concubines. Each of those women had children and it is clear that it was not all peace and joy in that family. In Genesis their quarrels and jealousies are clearly described. In Genesis 37:4 it is stated that Joseph's brothers hated him so badly that they could not even speak a kind word to him. Jacob however loved him more than any of his other children. In modern terms we would say that there was hatred, envy, jealousy, and preference of one above the other, from both parents and children. We certainly would not have placed them on our list of favourite Christian families! But was Joseph for ever afterwards hampered by his upbringing? No, he was one of the most outstanding and irreproachable figures of the Old Testament. He became a man with a blameless reputation, a noble character and great leadership qualities. We might exclaim, 'This cannot be possible with that kind of a background!' And yet, in God's grace it appears to be possible.

This is one of the very encouraging aspects of the Bible. The histories of these people are written down with an astonishing honesty. All their mistakes, failures, stupidities and sins are mentioned. And yet, God used them and permitted them to bring forth some outstanding children. This is a wonderful consolation for us, when our families are not perfect, even though we sometimes pretend they are. It is also a tremendous reassurance for those among us who struggle with serious family problems, or for the ones who stand alone after their partner has died or left.

If God is then so gracious towards the imperfections of our families, could we not try to be a little more gracious towards each other as well? Should we not give each other the freedom to have a slightly different opinion on some of these matters? I think that we would find this easier if we were convinced that the family is not the aim in itself, but a tool in God's hand to accomplish his work in this world.

A good and harmonious family certainly belongs to the most important matters in life. In our time there are few things that give such a strong testimony about God's saving and changing power in our lives, as a family where love and respect for each other are obvious. Therefore, the married woman will spend a lot of her time and energy in keeping her family 'happy', in raising her children and in serving the Lord in this way. But let us not make that fatal mistake of getting so preoccupied with the important matter of the family, that we lose sight of the most important matter in life . . . God himself.

Paul speaks of these matters in 1 Corinthians, when he reminds us that 'an unmarried woman . . . is concerned about the Lord's affairs: Her aim is to be devoted to the Lord in both body and spirit. But a married woman is concerned about the affairs of this world—how she can please her husband' (1 Corinthians 7:34). Then he goes on to emphasise that everything in this world is passing, and how true this is for the family. Suddenly you realise that your children are grown up, and once they begin to leave home, things change very quickly. If all your priorities have been centred around your family, you quickly realise that you are left behind with empty hands. However, if God and your service to him was the centre of your life, you might have some adapting to do, but you have not lost the aim of your life. With God's help and some alterations in your programme, you will make it.

Jonathan, our eldest son, has been gone for many years now. He left for the United States to study at a Bible College, and he got married. We always had a strong feeling of comradeship and friendship with him. He's gone now, but those ties and feelings have definitely not weakened. We love him and his wife very much, and would love having them with us, but we have been able to adjust quite easily to this new situation. Now the next three are on the verge of leaving as well, which will mean another time of adaptation for us. I do believe that our common love for God and his work in this world plays a big role in all this. We have been and will remain united in that aim, even when we are separated by thousands of miles. God will be here and he will be there and he alone will satisfy the needs of our lives, as we continue to give him the first place.

Built on the rock

Whenever I read about the wise man and the foolish man, I am deeply touched by the words of the Lord Jesus. The wise man, who built his house on a rock, was the one who heard his words and *obeyed* them. When the storms of life came and beat upon the house, it did not fall.

When I read this parable, I cannot help but think of Marrie. Marrie and her husband Joop had already worked for several years on a very difficult mission field, where the message of the gospel was being opposed by fanatics. Suddenly a special opportunity to obtain a visa for a longer period was offered to them. This would enable them to settle in a town where there was great spiritual pressure. Only a few months earlier a friend of theirs had been murdered in that same town, so Marrie and Joop knew the risks involved. They nevertheless decided to accept the challenge.

The months that followed were not easy but they remained optimistic. But then tragedy struck. While sleeping one night, Joop had a convulsion and died within minutes. We were deeply shocked when we received this news the next morning. I will never forget the reaction of a friend, who was very close to Marrie, and had grown up with her. She said: 'I was relieved when I heard it concerned Joop and Marrie. If there is one person who will be able to cope gloriously, with God's help, it is Marrie. When she was a young girl, all her love, dedication and time was for the Lord Jesus. Also later, as a wife and mother, she always kept a close relationship with the Lord Jesus. My heart is bleeding for Marrie in her time of grief, but I am sure she will make it.'

Marrie pulled through. It was not easy to bury her husband in that far-away country and to come back alone with two small children. The lonely weeks and months that followed were not easy either, but her testimony was clear and gave glory to God. Each time I spoke with her I was deeply touched and encouraged and many others shared a similar experience. Marrie had built her house on the rock. When the gale struck with great force, her house stood firm. Today Marrie is married to another fine Christian and they are back on the mission field.

Many of us are more often like the foolish man. We hear the words of the Lord, but do not act upon them. As a result, when the storm comes, our house will fall. The Lord said: 'And it fell with a great crash.' This is a solemn warning. In the next few chapters we will look at how we can apply our dedication to Christ in a practical way in our everyday life. But before we can apply anything, we must be dedicated! This is a decision only *you* can take!

3

Ordering Your Daily Life

We have seen that the biblical vision for women is both broad and encouraging, and the claims God makes on our lives are enormous. This indicates an exciting adventure if we are prepared to get serious with and about God. But I also know from experience just how depressing such adventures can be. Often we feel like failures, and that we haven't really achieved anything of note. It seems as if a great wall has been built before us, hindering us from doing something really useful.

Often such hindrances are of a practical nature, but are still difficult to overcome. When I study the activity list of our friend in Proverbs 31, I come to the conclusion she was well-organised. She simply had to be, otherwise she would have made a mess of things. I know most of us don't have the natural ability to organise, especially in our personal lives, but working to a specific schedule, programme or goal is something we have to develop and work at.

Of course, we are all different, and one person does seem more organised than the next, but I believe it is in our sinful nature to organise in a slapdash way! Sin is often described as 'missing the mark'. Ever since sin has come into this world, humanity has specialised in missing not only God's mark, but also in missing the mark in day-to-day activities. How often do we just leave things to our 'feelings'? If the sun shines today we feel like cleaning the windows. If it shines again a week later, we rather feel like sitting in the garden, lapping it up. And when it rains, we normally feel like staying in bed all day. Can you imagine what the world would have been like if everybody lived by their feelings? It is obvious our feelings are unreliable advisors.

It could also be that we have learned to organise certain areas in our life and left others untouched, either by lack of necessity or lack of interest in that area of our life. When I was still studying, we were virtually forced to organise our time wisely, and this has stood me in good stead. If you don't learn to organise in that time of life between the ages of six years and eighteen or twenty-five, the result will be bad grades, academic failure and everything that goes with it.

The area of housekeeping, family and related issues is a completely different aspect of our life. An area which most of us develop rather reluctantly, I'm sure, some time after our twentieth birthday! It isn't really interesting and is not compulsory like school...but it is an important part of every woman's life, married or single, whether we like it or not! Just the other day I read that a woman who wants to scale new heights needs more organisation in her life than a man...because she doesn't have a wife at home to do it for her!

Time for God

First let's give our attention to the top priority of our lives; our time with God. If we do nothing about this, we can be sure that nothing will be the result. All the practical details of life are screaming for attention and we still have to do the shopping, cooking and washing, whether we like it or not. God and his Word can easily be forgot-

ten if we are not careful about it. In the parable of the
sower Jesus reminds us that part of the seed that is sown
(meaning God's Word), is choked by the worries of this
life and the deceitfulness of wealth, and so it does not
bear fruit. I have found that the worries of this life are an
enormous hindrance in the spiritual life of many women.
Therefore, we *have* to *make* time for God and his Word,
whatever our schedule may be. The woman of Proverbs
31 was also extremely busy and yet she gave God the pre-
eminent place in her life!

This comes down to a decision again. Am I really
convinced that I need God that much? Do I really
believe in the importance of Bible study and prayer in
order to attain that change of character? Then I have to
sit down and reconsider my schedule in order to decide
what is the best time of the day to give to God. And
when that is settled I have to take a second decision in
which I resolve to do my utmost to stick to that time and
progress in my daily walk with God.

And what if I fail and do not have my time with God
for days or even weeks at a time? In that case I will not
be helped by vague feelings of guilt or spiritual
inferiority. Only a fresh decision to give it another go
will help me to get back on the right track. Probably
every Christian woman would love to become like our
friend in Proverbs 31. The only way to achieve that goal
is to follow the road of clear decisions and planning.
That planning has to be reviewed regularly however, as
our lives are not static, but changing constantly by the
influence of many factors around us.

For example, maybe I decided at the beginning of one
year to reserve the time after lunch for Bible study and
prayer. In that hour in the early afternoon, the bigger
children were still in school and the little ones were
taking a nap. I also decided that Thursday nights would
be dedicated to the reading of good books or listening to

tapes, because that was the night my husband had some meeting or other. But the next year all that was changed. Maybe the younger children no longer slept in the afternoon, but went to bed earlier instead, so that I was then able to have my times of devotion in the morning, while Tuesday nights became the time I listened to tapes or read books. We must be flexible. It is very important to review our schedule regularly, and adjust it as seems necessary. Another important matter is to get yourself some good aids to stimulate your study.

Every woman needs encouragement in the form of a regular church service, fellowship-group meeting or prayer meeting. In some periods of a woman's life, especially when you've just had a baby and while the children are still small, you become limited in the extent to which you may be involved in God's work. But no matter how small your contribution, just be involved! Look frantically for every possible opportunity to attend some kind of Christian meeting, and find solutions to those things keeping you from doing just that. Don't automatically think that your husband is the one who should go to every meeting, while you stay at home with the children. Your spiritual life is of great importance for the well-being of the whole family!

Organising your time

We have already seen that the woman in Proverbs 31 was extremely well-organised in all aspects of her life. Sometimes, as we read through this chapter, the conviction becomes stronger that we fall far short of the women God wants us to be. How can we move from those beds while it is still dark? It's difficult enough to get out of bed when the sun is already shining brightly! How can we be expected to find time to help the poor and the needy, when it's virtually impossible for us to cope with our own households? How can the new day be met with joy and laughter when you have been up most of the night with a sick child? And as for the words of wisdom and instruction that should always be on our tongue...well, maybe we should not think too closely about that one.

Some years ago we took a trip to Spain with our growing family, and we were asked to take along two English girls, so that they could learn some Spanish. We travelled a few thousand miles and saw just about every inch of the country, but when we got home six weeks later, the girls hadn't learned any Spanish at all. But they had learned some Dutch! They had quickly grasped phrases like 'hou je mond' and 'zit stil' (shut up and sit still), which were evidently what they had heard most often on the trip. I was of course horrified at these 'words of wisdom' that they had heard from *my* mouth...

Fortunately we have the opportunity to change our lives. When I married at the age of twenty-two, I was the classical example of a girl who was extremely well-organised in some things, but did not have the slightest notion of housekeeping. I remember the evaluation different teachers had to write about us at the Bible school where I studied. In most areas, like diligence, friendliness, helpfulness and devotion, their judgements were quite unanimous about me. But I laughed quite a bit about their evaluations with regard to my 'orderliness, neatness and self-discipline'! I couldn't understand all of this, but what it did prove to me at that age was that these character evaluations were useless. Various teachers, who knew me only as a student in their class, gave me the highest grades for orderliness and neatness. The people, on the other hand, who guided me in my housekeeping efforts held a totally different opinion...and gave me the lowest scores!

When I started my life as a housewife shortly afterwards, and had to deal with things other than church history and theology, I discovered—to my regret—that both parties were correct in their evaluation of my orderliness and neatness. Because of this the first four years of my marriage were not really examples of 'how it should be done'. In my defence I have to say I had difficult pregnancies. With the first I had morning sickness for nine months, and with my second pregnancy I was bedridden for four months because of the danger of a possible miscarriage. None of this in any way contributed to me getting my housekeeping going! But I also totally lacked knowledge of how to 'attack' my housekeeping rationally and with skill. The thought that this was possible never even occurred to me. All I can remember from those four years is that I didn't cope. Often at twelve noon I was still walking around in my nightgown with uncombed hair, the baby bath with all the things around it still in the living room (the only place where we had a stove), the breakfast dishes still in the kitchen, aware that I had to start peeling potatoes, but the baby had started crying again, and then Kees came home with an unexpected visitor! What misery! What humiliation!

The move to Louvain and our introduction to full-time work with Operation Mobilisation (OM) brought a radical change to my life. We rented an enormous house on the Schreursvest and started living with a team of young people. Rooms in the cellar were converted into offices. The ground floor was general living space for all of us with a living room, a dining room and a big kitchen. All the girls slept in the two bedrooms on the first floor. We lived on the second floor in two bedrooms, first with four Rosies, later with five. The young men on the team slept on the third floor. We started our ministry in Louvain with a big evangelistic outreach that lasted two

months and in which regularly up to fifty people partici-
pated. All the girls slept in our house and the young men
in a little garden house and in a student building we had
rented. Everybody ate with us and our house was the
centre of all activity. Needless to say a small revolution
in my housekeeping and organisational ability had to
take place to avoid having a disaster on our hands!

I must say that, out of necessity and sheer despera-
tion, I learned very quickly and made more progress
during one month in Louvain than in the first four years.
I had to be dressed, washed and combed before breakfast. If I had not made the beds before I went down, I
would not have any time to do it later. Since our bed-
room also served as our living room where we often had
meetings, the bed had to be made, the dirty socks
removed and the whole area ready for action by eight
o'clock in the morning. To my great surprise, when I *had*
to do it, it worked, and it gave great satisfaction that
everything was done so early in the morning. The three
years I spent as housemother of a team of about twenty
people, with the additional responsibility of caring for
my own family, taught me to organise my household
thoroughly, work with lists and to delegate jobs. When
we started living on our own again after three years, I
discovered that, thanks to my newly acquired organisational ability, I had a lot of time left for other things.

Circumstances forced me to drastically change my
approach to housekeeping. But how can you do this
when nothing forces you? Where there's a will there's a
way! It's horrible living in chaos all your life. Through
the years I have talked to many young women who were
wrestling with the same problems. When they talked or
wrote to me about it, it was always accompanied with a
feeling of shame and failure. If you know you have
problems in this area, stop feeling ashamed and stop

complaining about it, but decide to start doing something about it.

My first golden rule is: make a good start! Don't waste your time in the morning. The breakfast dishes don't automatically walk to the sink or the dishwasher. They need to be taken there! Don't sit down with the newspaper and the post, but *do* something. Help yourself to get going by switching on some nice music or having a cup of strong coffee, but then start! Take care that the most important things are out of the way, like clearing the breakfast table, doing the dishes, making the beds and putting the laundry in the machine. You will feel a totally different person when the house is more or less in order and if somebody should drop in, it looks a lot more attractive.

Another golden rule is: finish what you start! If you don't clear the table properly, forget to fill the washing-machine, then realise you actually wanted to wash your hair, but on the way to the bathroom quickly make the beds, by ten o'clock you will be still walking around the house half dressed, with wet hair and the house in a bigger mess than before. Discipline yourself in this, and if you find it difficult give yourself a reward after each completed task! For example, promise yourself: 'When the dishes are done, the beds made and the living room hoovered, I'll make a cup of coffee!' It might sound stupid and silly, but it works.

If you want to clean your house properly, divide your work systematically. Take a few rooms per day. This is my schedule:

Monday: Kitchen, toilet, a good cleaning of the playroom, hoovering the living room, the laundry.

Tuesday: Hand laundry, time for visiting, special shopping, study.

Wednesday: Bedrooms, stairs, bathroom (possibly wash a few windows upstairs). In the afternoon time with the children.

Thursday: Ironing, correspondence, study/writing.

Friday: Clean the rooms, wash windows, clean the corridor, shopping in the afternoon for the whole week.

Saturday: Prepare the food for the weekend.

It's not so easy for something to go wrong if you're working to a schedule. Make sure you stick to it! Allow yourself only in extreme cases, for example in sickness, to change your plan. Try to stay on top of the work, don't let the work start ruling you. After your meal, do the dishes immediately. Do the laundry regularly. Don't let it become a discouraging bundle! Once you're in control, housekeeping can be quite pleasant.

Of course this particular schedule would not be suitable for everyone. If you have a new-born baby, for example, you may find yourself living in chaos for a few months, or if you are a working mother, your schedule will have to be a lot tighter. But whatever your situation, work out some sort of schedule.

You might find this strange, but it's good to even plan your menu for the week. It will just take half an hour. It is also easier then to draw up a shopping list, and so you can do the week's shopping in one afternoon. By having a set menu, you'll find yourself making a wider variety of dishes, and you will eliminate the duplication of dishes. You won't grow old so quickly either, because you don't have to worry about deciding what you're going to cook each day. When you are planning your menu, take some time to glance through a cookery book, or magazines with recipes. Then you just add the needed ingredients to your shopping list. I know most people don't like working with lists, but in this case it certainly has its advantages. Because you have decided beforehand what to buy, it is more difficult to be influenced by things that are being advertised in the shop, and so you'll save money.

When you make your job list for the house, remember to delegate tasks to other members of the family. It won't just lighten your load, but at the same you will be teaching them to handle some responsibility. Our children have been taught to make their beds before they come for breakfast. They're also expected to keep their own rooms tidy, and together we are responsible for the evening dishes. When they were little it took quite a bit of effort on our part to teach them this! The reward system that James Dobson mentions in his book *Dare To Discipline* was a real help to me. Today it is all a matter of routine which nobody changes unless something very unusual takes place. It is important to realise the necessity of having your housekeeping under control before you can do something else. So take it seriously!

Organising your body—keeping fit!

Our friend in Proverbs 31 has another side to her life as well; 'She sets about her work vigorously; her arms are strong for her tasks' (verse 17) 'She is clothed with strength and dignity; she can laugh at the days to come' (verse 25). When I read how she strengthens her arms I can't help but think of an attractive Arab Christian woman I met. She was young, beautiful and newly married. During one of our conversations, she lifted her slim arm and proudly remarked; 'I do body-building.'

Of course what we do to keep fit is not the issue. Being strong is affected by our emotional and spiritual life, but it remains true that power and strength, and the ability to face the next day with anticipation, has a physical side which is lacking in many women today. Many times we hear women say; 'I am so tired!', and often it is not those who do most who say this, but those who do least.

Reading the accomplishments of the Proverbs 31 woman sets one thinking: 'How does she keep this up?' Undoubtedly an efficient organising of her time plays an important part. It is also important to know the limits of your own physical strength and to stick to that. Just this week I told a friend that I was very busy and felt extremely tired. She replied: 'I can't sympathise because I don't know the feeling.' One woman has more physical reserves than another. There is no way we can compare ourselves with others. We simply have to learn what our limitations are. The right amount of sleep is important in order to function well during the day. Sometimes we only feel physically and spiritually miserable because we haven't been sleeping too well for the past few weeks.

To keep our bodies fit through healthy eating and exercises is also vital. A couple of years ago I thought I was developing some heart problems, and went to see a specialist. His response was; 'Your heart is okay, but the general condition of your body is bad. You need exercise.' I have never been a morning person and so, in the afternoons, I went to the 'trim-park' in the woods of Heverlee. I started to enjoy it, and after a while I noticed an improvement in my physical condition.

For quite a while I have been suffering from rheumatic pains and when I first started running it was not very easy. However, a couple of years ago, on a beautiful spring morning, I started running early in the morning and to my surprise I really enjoyed it. For some years now Kees and I have continued to run early in the morning and I must say that I feel a thousand times better than I have felt for years. After my run in the morning I have much more energy to accomplish my work, because I am warmed up and the blood circulates better. My rheumatic complaints have disappeared almost completely and I sleep a lot better. To put it simply; the exercise has done me the world of good, and my ability to last a full day has improved.

I realise that not everybody can go running. But I am sure there is some kind of sport that suits you and which you like: swimming, cycling, tennis, aerobics, jazz-ballet, squash, volleyball, and so on. What is important is to get fit, and stay that way. You are never too old to start. I only started when I was forty and last week I heard about a fifty-year-old woman who replaced her son in a marathon and finished last. This became such a challenge to her that she decided to start training. After three years she had accomplished so much that she was able to take part in a number of races, and even won some. She even set some veteran records! And she only started after she was fifty! But even if you will never be able to run a marathon, it is still important to do something to stay physically fit. Besides being in better physical shape, you will relax much more easily, and be a much happier person.

You can also combine your desire to get fit with sharing your faith. By joining a sports club, you automatically come into contact with other women, which can then lead to you sharing your faith with them. We so easily become used to just moving in Christian circles, our church or our Bible-study group. By being involved in 'something else' you can combine getting fit with witnessing. If your concern is that your husband won't approve, or that you will be spending less time with the family, you can choose a sport in which the whole family can be involved.

When our children were small, it was customary to go swimming every Saturday. On Sundays we went for long walks in the woods, or we went cycling. Now that our kids are much bigger, they have started playing squash.

So Kees and I had to try and master this sport. At first I struggled quite a bit, but after about ten lessons I felt much more confident about my game. We play twice a week with whoever is available. Besides improving our physical condition, we're also enhancing family relationships. While learning to play squash, I lost quite a bit of my pride. My lessons were once a week from eleven till twelve, and this happened to coincide with the time my second son, Henno, was there with the rest of his class for their hour of sport. While I was trying my utmost to make contact with the ball, he would be watching with the rest of the class...a humiliating experience...but I did learn to play squash!

I know mothers who accompanied their daughters to jazz-ballet or aerobics and their comments were the same: 'Very good for your physical condition, great fun, enhances the mother-daughter relationship and it's useful for making contact with other women.'

'She sets about her work vigorously; her arms are strong for her tasks.' 'She is clothed with strength and dignity.' This is something we have to work at. It doesn't just happen! It's difficult to get away from the mentality of: 'I just can't cope', but working on our physical condition will help us to get well on our way.

Physical strength is very important, but only one side of the picture. To what extent you can 'cope' on the spiritual and emotional side is just as important, if not more important. People are made of body, soul and spirit and these are intertwined. Just examine yourself to see how cheerful and 'spiritual' you will feel when you have had stomach-ache all night. Lack of sleep can make us terribly depressed and irritable. Often we look for the reason why we are struggling spiritually, while a good sleep is all that's needed to solve the problem.

Then again, a person in good physical condition or

even a professional athlete, is not always in control spiritually or emotionally. How then do we become women of all-round strength and dignity? Is some good exercise all it takes? Certainly not! Have you noticed how a physically weak person can communicate spiritual and emotional strength? Think of Joni Eareckson in her wheelchair. Although we should not romanticise Joni's life or under-estimate her handicap, she is, in spite of her broken body, a woman who radiates strength and dignity. But more about this in the next chapter.

Taking action

If we devote ourselves in such a determined way to the aim of seeing our lives with God grow and unfold, we will be surprised to notice after some time that the fruit of the Spirit is becoming manifest in our lives and that we're beginning to look like the woman of Proverbs 31.

After discovering the spiritual source from which the woman draws her characteristics, I am amazed to find out how many times she takes the initiative. How is it possible that the 'ideal woman' is pictured in such a way, while the same Bible tells us in Ephesians 5 that a wife should be submissive in all things? Are these two portions of Scripture not in conflict with each other? I don't think so. Before we read anything else about her and her qualities, we do read something about her husband and the relationship there is between the two of them. In verses 11 and 12, we see that 'her husband has full confidence in her and lacks nothing of value. She brings him good, not harm, all the days of her life'.

Her husband has full confidence in her. He married a wonderful woman and he knows it. He is proud of her (verse 28) and he knows that he is an important part of everything she does. He is also an important figure. He is a member of the town council or perhaps even the national governing body (verse 23), and he does not feel threatened by his very capable and vivacious wife. he gladly gives her all the room she needs, and he knows that all her activities will only bring him good (verse 12).

I believe that this chapter shows us clearly that submission in marriage, in the true biblical sense, does not degrade a woman to the role of a housemaid, who jumps when her husband as much as snaps his fingers. In a biblical relationship of love and a submissive spirit there is so much scope for both! Each couple must find their own balance in their relationship, constantly seeking God's guidance. The balance found by those two people in their harmonious relationship gives her all the room she needs for her personal development, for initiative and decisions (and not only about what they will eat today). I think that the complete confidence her husband places in her, and the fact that he encourages and praises her, have contributed very much to her spiritual development.

Looking back over our twenty-five years of married life, I have to admit that most of the things I undertook—apart from my housekeeping—only started after my husband Kees encouraged me greatly and in some cases even persuaded me to try new things. An example from our younger years was certainly that Kees felt that I should learn to drive. I had had an unfortunate experience in earlier years, which had made me so scared that I would not even consider giving it another try. In the end Kees made me go to a driving school. It was the hardest of things for me to do, but, after just a few hours of driving, I began to enjoy it again, and was soon driving all over the place. My life with four small children and a husband who was often away became much easier and pleasant after I was able to get around by car. Since those days I have driven thousands of miles in many different countries and in many different cars. Without

Kees's persistent encouragement, I do not think I would ever have got so far.

Later on it was Kees's idea and encouragement that led me to begin to translate books from English and French into Dutch. This gave me my first experience in writing, which motivated me to write my own books. He also encouraged me very much to begin travelling for speaking engagements and to get some experience of different mission fields. Possibly in the end I might have started some of these things by myself, but at the time I was almost overwhelmed by all the demands that a young family puts on a mother and there was certainly no energy nor ambition left to try to venture out beyond the borders of that well-known world of my own home.

Since then, I have had many talks and discussions with women who admitted that they also preferred to stay in the safety and warm shelter of their home. It appears to be difficult to begin something new. The older you get, the harder it becomes. The risk of making blunders in that great, unknown and hostile world, seems to get bigger as you grow older. Yet many talents remain undiscovered and undeveloped in this way. It requires a wise, loving and confident husband who will encourage his wife right from the start to develop herself in those areas where she has most potential. Perhaps he will have to sacrifice, or even suffer, by doing the dishes from time to time. But in the end he will gain as well.

But what happens if your husband is not like that, and is not supportive of the idea that you explore and develop new areas in your life? Maybe his own mother never moved out from the world of her own home, and he is secretly afraid that if you do develop outside interests, your family life will suffer. This attitude does make it much more difficult, and you will probably have to limit yourself to doing only one new thing per year, but even this is better than nothing. If you carefully choose your new projects, so as not to make your husband feel threatened, then it should work out. Perhaps you can follow a Bible correspondence course, learn to drive, study a language by correspondence or tapes, or learn something that is obviously profitable to the whole family (like a cookery or sewing course). This might change your husband's ideas and help you to enlarge your boundaries gradually. After twenty years, you will see that you are nearly as versatile as our friend in Proverbs.

So we have seen that, after deciding our priorities, organising and planning are a vital part of our spiritual lives. Once our daily lives are ordered as much as possible, with time for God, time for practical activities, and time for relaxation and keeping fit, then we can start to tackle the spiritual and emotional aspects of our lives.

4

Discovering Your Spiritual Gifts

If we can believe the Bible (and I assume we do), then each of us has received specific gifts from God. You receive those gifts the moment you become a child of God and become part of his Body, the Church. Some people become aware of that immediately and start working with them. Others take a long, long time to discover them. Some of us never discover them.

The Bible very clearly shows us that we all receive spiritual gifts. In Romans 12:1–8 Paul makes the connection between offering your bodies as living sacrifices to God and an explanation of the different gifts in the Body of Christ, according to the grace given to us. This is God's own doing! Just as he took pleasure in the creation with all its variety and diversity, in which no cell or snowflake is the same, so he takes pleasure in distributing many gifts within the Body of Christ. Paul also emphasises this in 1 Corinthians 12. He even goes on to compare the different gifts in the Church with the parts of the human body.

Christians the world over have always thought: 'I can't do anything, I'm not important!' Paul fights this with very fundamental and logical arguments. Is the eye more important than the ear, or is it the job of the foot only to produce dirty socks? Of course not, that's crazy!

Paul says; 'Even our most important parts [for example our hearts, nervous systems and livers] are not visible and therefore receive no glory.' (Ever seen a heart with a bow or a vein with a diamond ring?) The most vital organs in our bodies don't need to be honoured. In our hair we wear ribbons, and our finger shows off a diamond ring. Still, if we're really forced to, we would be able to live without that finger and without that hair. Because it is visible to those around you, doesn't mean that it increases in importance. Every part of the body has a part to play, and it is for the good of the whole body that they all function properly. This holds true for both men and women.

Paul's arguments are clear and easy to understand. If the women have the idea that it is not meant for them, more than half of the Body of Christ would not function! Do you know what it means if half of the body does not function?

A very good friend of the family, Jonathan McRostie of Operation Mobilisation, knows only too well what this means. He had a serious car accident a few years ago in which he broke his neck and was paralysed from his chest down. This is one of the worst things that can happen to a person, when one half of your body no longer functions. Not only will you be limited in what you can do, but those paralysed parts become weak. One of the hardest aspects of such a handicap is perhaps that the person remains the same, while the body does not work! His attitude didn't change, his temperament is the same. Jonathan was always energetic, travelling all over the place, strong as a horse, didn't need much sleep and was always doing a thousand things at once. Now this same man sits in a wheelchair and more than half of his body cannot execute the commands given by his brain! A person with so many possibilities, but a body that can no longer function properly!

Let me take it a step further. The Lord Jesus is the head of the Body. He has many ideas, plans and perfect projects to execute in this world. But that Body! Half of it refuses to move! Many of the members only sit and grumble, indulging in self-pity. Another part of the body is too busy criticising those members that do function. Another part of the body is female—and believes that is enough reason not to function properly! It helps when you consider that Jesus sits at the right hand of the Father, a place where there is no frustration. I am sure the situation on earth saddens him.

The big question people ask time and time again is; 'How do I discover my spiritual gifts?'

1. You will have an inner conviction, recognising that this gift is meant for you. The Holy Spirit, given to you by God as a personal Counsellor, is the same Spirit who distributes the gifts (1 Corinthians 12:11)! Paul says in 1 Corinthians 2:12 that one of the reasons for us receiving the Holy Spirit is so that 'we may understand what God has freely given us'. That's great! God doesn't want us to be unsure about our gifts, he wants us to know what our gifts are, and he will have this recognition take place in our hearts through his Holy Spirit.

When I reflect on some of the women in our church who have the gift of serving, I discover that often they pop up in the right place at the right time. Sometimes to deliver flowers, hoover or just encourage. These seemingly unimportant services to friends, or people in need, give them great pleasure and satisfaction.

I think God has given me a gift for writing and speaking at meetings, seminars, and so on. When I started to teach Sunday School and address children's clubs shortly after my conversion, I began to enjoy relating stories. From a very young age I loved writing, and I go through writing letters at quite a rapid pace. I don't have to sit and think what I am going to write and I seldom have to start again. I see it as a real ministry to write letters to people on the mission field or to write a few words of encouragement to people who have difficulties.

Basically, we can say that you will experience an inner freedom, confirmation and fulfilment by exercising your gifts. We sometimes find it hard to believe that our gifts may involve those things which we enjoy doing. People sometimes see God as a spoilsport who wants us to do that which we hate most. Nothing could be further from the truth! God is a loving Father. The gifts he gives us are good, and it is his will that he be glorified through it all and that our joy may be full. But imagine if I had never been to school and never learned to write! How would I have known that writing was my gift?

2. *You will have to start doing things* in order to discover your gifts. You will never discover your gifts by sitting at home and wondering what they are! Endless prayers will not make you any the wiser concerning your gifts. You have to start experimenting and being involved. If you start teaching Sunday School, you could discover after a year that you do have a gift of teaching. But if you hadn't become involved, how would you have found out? If you have the gift of wisdom, you will have to start working with people and their problems before you will discover that God gave you a gift in that area. The gift of knowledge will without a doubt be accompanied by lots of study, meditation and reading before the knowledge comes to the surface in your contact with other people. I can give you endless illustrations. Gifts will only be clearly revealed when a person becomes available and starts accepting specific responsibilities. The more you become involved, the stronger the confirmation will be that this is your gift.

It is unfortunate that we sometimes have to do things

which certainly are not our gifts, because of a shortage of available and capable people. On completion of my studies at Bible College, I was asked to do the book-keeping of the Belgian Gospel Mission for three months. During my high school years in Den Helder I had studied a bit of book-keeping, and hated it! I simply failed to grasp the principles involved, and even though I had extra lessons, my grades were bad. Suddenly I had to do it for three months. Fortunately it was quite easy. It was a matter of completing lists and adding all the figures up. That I could do easily enough!

At the end of the three months I went to the office of our Director to be informed as to what my next job would be. I was sure that this time it would be something more in line with my gifts. Fat chance! It had been decided that because I did such a good job, I should do the book-keeping for a further nine months. I was absolutely furious, and after my protests failed, I burst into tears. It made no impression on the Director at all, and I simply had to do the job.

The situation got so bad that when Kees and I wanted to get married later that year (Kees had become pastor-evangelist in a small Belgian town), the mission board had to decide on the date to avoid it clashing with my duties as book-keeper. After long hours of negotiation we finally got permission to marry on 20 February, on condition that I would be in Brussels every day until 1 June, to do the book-keeping. I am still convinced that book-keeping is not my gift, but I learnt a lot during that year—patience, submission and a lot of compassion for those girls on our OM teams who have to do book-keeping, while not really wanting to either.

Sometimes it is necessary for us to do these things, in order for God to teach us something else. On the other hand, we can also say that by being available to do whatever we are called upon to do, we can discover our

gifts much more quickly. But what if you're convinced
that you are gifted in a certain area, and everybody else
fails to realise this?

3. *Ask a mature fellow-Christian* for his/her honest opinion on your gifts. It's possible for us to make mistakes.
There are people who always think less about themselves
and who would never dare to accept that certain qualities
are given to them by God as gifts. If they took the liberty
of asking another Christian's opinion, a whole new world
would open up for them. People with inferiority complexes and feelings of insecurity fall into this category.
It's possible that they were always taught that humility is
one of life's great virtues, and for fear of becoming
proud, they fail to recognise and exercise their gifts.

There is a role that we can play in helping others to
discover their gifts. Especially if people are modest,
young or inexperienced, it would be a great help if an
older, more mature Christian could discuss the subject of
gifts with them, and help them discover theirs. I think
that this is an important task especially for youth leaders,
pastors and leaders of Bible study groups. Even among
friends, in a home fellowship group or a prayer meeting
at work, it is good, and biblical, to encourage one
another. It's easy for you to see certain abilities you have
as your gift, while a more mature Christian would spot
something in you which never crossed your mind.

I received a letter from my sister saying that I clearly
had the gift of 'hospitality'. If I had made a list of my
gifts, that certainly wouldn't have been on it. My sister,
her husband and their three children work in the Middle
East, and had just spent a few months in Europe. During
this time they stayed with us for quite a while. Even
though it meant an extra work-load, especially with
more children around, we thoroughly enjoyed the time
together. We saw it as simply our duty to offer them a

home. My sister obviously saw in us the gift of 'hospitality', and confirmed it with the words; 'We really felt at home.' I must say that her words not only surprised me, but also encouraged me. Hospitality is a gift we find in the Bible (Romans 12:13), a gift we have to exercise without grumbling (1 Peter 4:9) and which is a condition for someone in church leadership (Titus 1:8). My sister's words encouraged me to look at this gift in a new way. If this was one of our gifts, then as we exercised it God would bless us. A couple of years later, when we were flooded with guests for a long period, I sometimes had the feeling that it was all too much. But the knowledge that others had noticed this gift helped and motivated me to keep going.

Let's draw attention to one another's gifts. Spiritually this can be such an encouragement! It can release such boldness through which a modest person will start exercising a precious gift with thankfulness. It will help to overcome inferiority complexes. It will be useful for many, many people and God will be glorified through it all.

But the opposite is also true! Paul seriously warns us: 'Do not think of yourselves more highly than you ought' (Romans 12:3). He also says in Galatians 6:3: 'If anyone thinks he is something when he is nothing, he deceives himself.' That is the other side of the coin! Sometimes we need somebody who tells us honestly what we can do, but sometimes we also have to accept that others observe that a certain thing is not our gift. This is not easy, but can prevent lots of misery later on. It is not an easy task to approach a person and tell him that a particular thing he is doing is not his gift. I think you can only say this after a lot of thought and prayer. It also has to be done with much love and in humility. It is never nice to hear that it would be better not to do something. If it is said in love, and you know it does not concern your whole personality, then it is possible to accept this as something from the Lord.

We have experienced several times that when we hesitantly, being careful not to hurt, but inwardly convinced that this was something we had to do, suggested to someone that his gifts were not in leading a team or student evangelism, we have usually discovered to our surprise that the person in question was relieved to hear this. In his heart he was already convinced that this was not 'his gift'. His commitment to Jesus and willingness to be available had made him press on. An open and honest discussion about this then brought a breakthrough. It can be a tremendous burden to daily perform a task for which you are not equipped. That's why spiritual leaders need a lot of wisdom and insight in order to divide the tasks among the people concerned so that everybody is able to develop their gifts and to work in those areas for which God has called them. Young people should regularly ask for the advice of a more mature Christian.

The confirmation and joy the Holy Spirit will bring into your heart when you start doing the right things, together with the supporting advice of Christians who know you well, will make it clear what your gifts are. It is important to know your gifts. It is even biblical to reach out for the gifts of the Spirit. It will also give you a measure of peace and assurance when deciding what you have to do and what not. It will help you to serve the Lord and his Body with conviction in the right function. Do you know your gifts? No? Start discovering them according to the principles you have just read. You do know your gifts? Hurray! Thank the Lord for them. Never forget that they are gifts given by the Father from whom comes every gift that is good and perfect. Don't keep the gifts for yourself, start working with them in order that the Body can function and his name can be glorified!

5

Following God's Will

'Seek and you will find!' we snap, when Dad has mislaid
the car keys or one of the children has lost a glove. But
when Jesus spoke these words he was not referring to
our car keys. He was speaking about prayer and wanted
to teach us an important spiritual lesson. 'Ask and it will
be given to you; seek and you will find; knock and the
door will be opened to you' (Matthew 7:7). These words
were spoken by the Lord Jesus in an extraordinary message on basic spiritual principles which we know as 'The
Sermon on the Mount' or 'The Beatitudes'. Jesus wanted
the disciples, and us, to realise that God hears and
answers our prayers. He repeats this point three times,
using a different illustration on each occasion: he who
asks, shall receive; he who seeks, shall find; he who
knocks, shall have the door opened to him.

God is faithful and it does not please him that we
should be kept in suspense, patiently waiting for his
'secret will' to be revealed to us. In his great love for us,
God wants us to take the initiative and ask. He then
responds and gives, freely and in abundance.

Jesus stresses this point by comparing God to an
earthly father. When your child is hungry and asks for
bread, you do not give him a stone. If he would like a
fish, you do not give him a snake. All normal parents,

despite our sinful human nature, want to provide whatever is good and necessary for their children, as soon as
they possibly can. How much more then will our heavenly Father, who is sinless and perfect, answer the
prayers of his children!

Many Christians believe, however, that it is extremely
difficult to know the will of God for their lives. They
pray for months and years without God's will ever being
revealed to them and achieve nothing because they are
too afraid to take the initiative and become involved in
something. Precious years go by and are wasted while
they 'wait upon the Lord'. I believe that this approach is
not biblical. Concerning spiritual matters, the teachings
of Jesus are very clear, not to be misunderstood and
certainly not to be pushed aside: he who seeks, shall
find! Before we can discover the will of God, we should
consider some important basic principles:

1. *God is a loving Father* who delights in giving good
things to his children. Psalm 37:4,5 teaches: 'Delight
yourself in the Lord and he will give you the desires of
your heart. Commit your way to the Lord; trust in him
and he will do this.' Many people live with the strange
supposition that it is dangerous to know God's will for
your life because you never know what's in store for you.
I call this the 'bogeyman syndrome'. These people
reason as follows: 'I am really scared of flying, I can't
stand the heat, I love my family very much, my greatest
fears are snakes and scorpions...therefore, God will
send me to the heart of Africa as a missionary!' This is a
distorted image of God. He is good, he loves us and
delights in granting us the desires of our heart.

2. *God forgives and restores*. This willingness to forgive
is an outstanding characteristic of God. God forgives us
unconditionally over and over again. If we make a mis-

take and make the wrong choice, or fall into sin, we need
to repent and confess and there is immediate forgiveness
and restoration (think of David in 2 Samuel 12:13).

Many people are afraid to take a decision one way or
the other for fear of being way out of line with what God
wants for their lives. Do you think this fits into God's
character of goodness and forgiveness? If a person ear-
nestly seeks God's will, but makes a wrong decision, do
you think God will write him off? God doesn't reason
like man. He won't say: 'Well, I wanted her to choose B,
but she went and chose A, so she is on her own now. I
don't want anything to do with her.' Does that sound like
the God we have come to know and love? Of course not.
God is full of mercy. He knows what we are made of! He
even extends his goodness further than we could ever
imagine.

God sent Jonah to Nineveh. But Jonah did not want
to go! Jonah knew God's will, but he didn't want to go!
This is of course even worse than accidentally making a
wrong decision. Jonah knew what God wanted him to
do, but he decided to go the other way. God allows him
to enjoy himself a little on his Mediterranean cruise, but
then brings him back. God takes him to Nineveh and
uses Jonah to save a whole city from total destruction—
despite his initial disobedience. God takes it even a step
further! When Jonah is confused and unhappy with God
and seeks some shade, God allows a tree to grow for him
to 'ease his discomfort' (Jonah 4:6). Don't you think this
is beautiful? God in his patience continues to work in the
life of an intentionally disobedient child. This is more
than we could ever dream of! Would he then leave us in
the cold if we honestly seek his will? Would he punish us
if we made one wrong decision? Of course not. God is a
Father. God loves us even as an earthly father loves his
own child. 'Second best' is not mentioned in the Bible.

Another beautiful example of restoration after a

wrong decision had been made is the story of John Mark. In Acts 15:35–41 we read that Paul and Barnabas start quarrelling about this boy. The apostles had taken him on their first missionary journey as Barnabas's nephew. What exactly happened we don't know, but it is clear that, halfway through the journey, this young man got fed up and went back to his mother. From Paul's fierce reaction to the whole situation we can assume that this was probably a stupid thing to do. Paul feels that John Mark has really wrecked the whole thing and refuses to take him on another missionary journey. The situation gets completely out of hand, Paul and Barnabas quarrel, and then decide that they will each go their separate ways. Thus John Mark's 'wrong' decision has far-reaching consequences.

But God clearly has more patience and understanding than Paul. Barnabas (whose name means 'son of comfort') takes the 'failure' under his wing. We discover later that John Mark was very useful in the ministry of the gospel and even to Paul (2 Timothy 4:11). In the end God gave him the honour of writing Mark's Gospel! Are you afraid to make the wrong decision? Read the Bible and let it change your image of God through the Holy Spirit. 'The Lord is compassionate and gracious, slow to anger, abounding in love' (Psalm 103:8).

3. We don't need divine guidance for everything we do. God has equipped us with something called common sense. I'm always amused when I read Paul's remark: 'Brothers, stop thinking like children. In regard to evil be infants, but in your thinking be adults!' (1 Corinthians 14:20). God has given us free will and our intellect and in the routine happenings of daily life he wants us to use our common sense and make decisions. I remember when I was a young Christian and everything was new and wonderful and I became aware that God wanted to guide me. I was terrified of doing something that could have been out of line with the will of God. Every time I was on my bicycle in Den Helder and came to a crossing, I was in the midst of a new conflict because I wasn't sure whether to go left or right. I could get to where I was going via any street, but the great question was: 'Which way did God want me to go?' I simply got off my bike and asked him. I soon realised how stupid this was, and that it was complicating my life unnecessarily. I realised that if I continued in this vein, I wouldn't get anywhere. Some time after that I met other young people who experienced the same difficulty. They were also searching for 'divine confirmation' in everything they were doing.

When I look back now I see how foolish it was. What did God give us brains for? Don't you think he expects us to make good use of them? When you read the book of Acts, you will see that Paul also planned using basic common sense—even for missionary journeys. If God had a different plan, don't you think he would reveal it if we are sensitive to the Holy Spirit? Use your common sense, take the best decision possible and know that the Lord is with you. If he wants to divert you, he will make that very clear.

I was also always afraid that if I went down one road, I would possibly miss someone that God wanted me to meet on the other road. But I have learnt. If God wants me to meet someone, he will definitely see to it that I do just that. Most of my unusual encounters in life took place when I least expected it.

One of the most striking examples was when Kees and I went to Switzerland by train for a week's holiday. Early one morning we sat in a local train opposite a young Japanese businessman in an immaculate dark grey suit, white shirt, tie, beautiful black shoes and a briefcase, who was on his way to Jungfrau Joch. At first we laughed a bit about him, but when we saw how nervous he was and that he had no idea how to get there, we felt sorry for him and then spoke to him in English. We helped him to change trains in Lauterbrunnen to Jungfrau Joch, the highest spot you can reach in the Alps.

Throughout the day, during our walks, we continually glanced up to the majestic snow-covered mountain peaks of Jungfrau wondering how he was doing in his black shiny shoes. You can only imagine how surprised we were when we met him on the train late that night. He had a wonderful day and we parted like old friends. Three days later and three hundred kilometres further, we sat in a train in the area of Zürich, when our Japanese friend entered our compartment again. We just couldn't believe it and the first quarter of an hour we spent laughing. He then showed us pictures of his wife and children and still laughing we speculated on how and where we would meet the next day. We told him it couldn't happen because we were leaving for Louvain the next day. His mouth fell open. He was flying to Brussels the next day to visit a factory between Brussels and Louvain. We gave him our address and phone number and lo and behold the next evening he was on our doorstep, just in time for supper.

Throughout the whole evening we were able to share our faith with him. He was a Buddhist and was looking for direction in life. We gave him some English books written by a Japanese lady who had become a Christian. He was genuinely interested and must have said about ten times: 'We didn't meet just by chance. God planned this!' We were naturally bowled over by all this, and also felt convinced that God had indeed brought us together. We have since lost touch with him, but a beautiful vase from Japan reminds us to pray for him. It had been an ordinary holiday, planned with some common sense. We didn't pray for hours before deciding which train to take. But God had a plan.

I could go on and on about this, and tell you many stories about how God uses our initiative. I am convinced that although our lives are totally dependent on God, he allows us to use our brains and to lead normal lives.

Conditions for God to reveal his will

There are occasions in life when we do need God's special guidance. But God sets us certain conditions before revealing his will for our lives.

1. We must be in a right relationship with God before we can start to understand God's ways. In Psalm 32:1–7, David talks about the necessity to confess your sins before God. 'Then I acknowledged my sin to you and did not cover up my iniquity. I said, "I will confess my transgressions to the Lord"—and you forgave the guilt of my sin' (verse 5). Following David's humbling of himself and confessing to God, God makes a promise: 'I will instruct you and teach you in the way you should go; I will counsel you and watch over you' (verse 8). Is that not exactly what we are looking for and that which we need in our lives, which can sometimes be so complicated? God wants to instruct us, teach and counsel us, but the first and most important condition is that we come to him in dependency and awareness of our guilt in order to heal the relationship between him and us.

In Romans 8 Paul speaks about the same things in a different way. He shows us that we can only be guided by God if we have become sons (or daughters) of him and have received his Holy Spirit in our lives (Romans 8:14, 15). If we don't belong to God then we have not received his Spirit and cannot accept and understand what God wants from us (Romans 8:5–9). The most important and most elementary condition to know God's will is that we have to become his children, that we receive his Spirit and, through confession of sin and dependency on him, keep our daily relationship with God open and honest.

2. We must be obedient to that which God has clearly revealed to us in his Word. For example, God hates adultery. The Bible shows that very clearly. As long as David was disobedient to this commandment, God wasn't able to do anything with and through him. Instead of experiencing God's guidance, he experienced God's hand heavy upon him (Psalm 32:4). Only after he confessed this sin was God able to continue to give guidance to his life. The Lord Jesus himself showed us the very close connection between keeping his commandments and a further revelation of himself in our life (John 14:21–24). It is impossible on the one hand to say that we love the Lord Jesus and want to follow him, while on the other hand we don't do what he has clearly commanded us to do. Obedience to that which we know is a 'must' in order to know God's will in those things that are not so clear.

3. We must be dedicated to God. In Romans 12:1,2 Paul urges us to offer our bodies as living sacrifices, holy and pleasing to God. The renewal of our mind that will take place through this dedication will enable us to learn to know the will of God.

4. We must ask God for his guidance. 'Lord, teach me your ways, show me your paths', is one of David's prayers which we find repeated regularly in the Psalms. But it is even much earlier in history that we see God answer prayers in a wonderful way—the prayers of his children asking for guidance.

When Abraham gives an exceptionally difficult task to his chief servant to go to his native country and to find a wife for his son Isaac, the servant realises that he needs God's guidance in this. He starts the journey to the country where he is going to find the girl. He chooses the best spot and the best time for this undertaking—the well outside town towards the evening. All the girls from the surrounding area will gather there to draw water. Up to that moment he follows his common sense. To make a choice though, he asks for God's guidance in a detailed description and God lets it happen that way. God's guidance is so striking, for the servant as well as for Rebekah and her family, that their reaction is one of deep respect and worship (Genesis 24).

God wants to guide us, sometimes even in a very personal way. This is a special privilege for God's children who enjoy and maintain an honest relationship with him.

How to find God's will?

1. By reading the Bible. 'Your word is a lamp to my feet and a light for my path' (Psalm 119:105). 'Your statutes are my delight; they are my counsellors' (Psalm 119:24). The Bible is a clear and concise medium through which God reveals his will. When I read the whole of Psalm 119, I'm amazed at the exceptional love David had for the Word of God, and the priority he gives to it. David was truly a man after God's heart. I think that his love for God's Word, and the way in which he applied it in his life, was the basis for the intimate relationship between him and God.

When we are busy studying the Bible, month after month and year after year, it will most certainly start to affect the decisions we make. A deep knowledge of God's Word will give us an assurance of knowing God's will. When we are occupied with God's Word then we will know about God's character, how he deals with things and what pleases and displeases him. A general and deep knowledge of God's Word is the first important way of God's leading. When a certain issue contradicts that which God has revealed to us in his Word, it cannot be his will; God does not contradict himself.

God can also speak to us clearly through a certain Bible verse which will guide us in our situation at that very moment. But here we have to be very cautious. It is easy to take verses out of context. By misinterpreting Scripture, you can let the Bible say anything you want it to. I remember when I was at Bible College and several of the young men approached the same girl with the intention of marriage. Each one of them were convinced that it was the will of God, and even had verses from Scripture to back them. The girl in question was quite self-conscious about the whole business. She didn't want to question God's Word, but she wasn't at all keen on any of them! To marry three men at the same time was also very complicated and according to Paul's teachings in the Bible and our European laws, could not be brought into accordance with God's revealed will! In the end she married someone totally different and all the above-mentioned men are now also happily married to other women.

When it fits our purpose, we can read all kind of answers into the Scriptures. Never forget that our hearts are cunning and we can really fool ourselves in these things. When you think the Lord is guiding you through a certain verse in the Bible, then first of all check if this is in accordance with the rest of the Bible. When you think it is, you can further test what you think is God's will until you are absolutely sure.

Several times in my life God has spoken to me through a specific verse. One of the most spectacular experiences in guidance we ever had was during the time we adopted our second daughter. Marlies, our first adopted daughter, was seven, and the two boys were ten and eight, when we began to think of adopting another girl. We started talking about this during a walk in the woods and all five of us were very enthusiastic about the idea. We had just received a small inheritance and what could be a better investment of the money than investing it in the life of a child? It would also be very nice for Marlies to have another sister from Korea as well as her blond brothers!

The adoption fever hit us. On Monday morning I immediately phoned the agency who had arranged the adoption of Marlies. Everything seemed to be fine. The papers would be sent to us that same day and if everything went smoothly, we would have another daughter within six months.

The papers were indeed in the postbox the next morning and we spent that evening filling them in thoroughly. The next day, though, I just couldn't bring myself to post them. Deep down inside of me I was disturbed. During the day I was all for it, but during the night I experienced many doubts. Night after night I lay awake for hours and my original enthusiasm changed into fear. What were we doing? We had asked for a child between four and six years old! The child would probably be difficult to handle, and it could ruin our lives. I wasn't sure how much I could handle. I was already too busy with Christian activities, evangelism, OM teams and I wasn't used to having small kids around any more. Why should I want to take on another small child who was possibly emotionally scarred after spending time in an orphanage?

As the nights went on my fear turned to panic! I tried to keep calm and wondered why I had never experienced these feelings when we were going through our first adoption. Was it merely because we were still young and inexperienced at that time? That might have been part of the reason. But with the first adoption we had something which seemingly was not working too well this time. With the adoption of Marlies we had the absolute assurance of God's guidance. In a miraculous way we suddenly received Marlies only two and a half months after filling in the forms. We knew people who had had their names on waiting lists for years. With Marlies we didn't have much money, and yet she was given to us even before we started paying adoption fees. In the first week God provided all the money we needed by way of gifts. No, the first time we were absolutely convinced that God had given us this child. But now? Now I wasn't sure at all. Now it just seemed like a nice idea and after a few days it didn't seem so nice any more. I realised that I needed God's clear guidance otherwise I wouldn't dare to start the adoption procedures again.

Just like Abraham's chief servant, and Gideon, I asked God that night for specific signs. We were dependent on gifts for our living and apart from the little bit of money out of the inheritance with which we could pay the adoption fees, we were not doing too well financially. This was another factor that made me doubt if it was right to adopt a child. I asked the Lord that night: 'Lord, if it is your will for us to adopt another child, please send in a gift for our family of five hundred guilders before Saturday.' We had never before received such a gift but when I started thinking about it, I decided to make it even more difficult, I prayed: 'Lord, give us one thousand guilders before Saturday. If we don't receive that money we will not adopt another child.' I was actually quite convinced that this would not happen. I was quite relieved after that, and soon fell asleep.

When the alarm went at seven o'clock the next morning, I took up my Bible. I followed a daily schedule and when I read the passage for that morning I got a big shock. The passage was from Titus 3:8: 'And I want you to stress these things, so that those who have trusted in God may be careful to devote themselves to doing what is good. These things are excellent and profitable for everyone.' During my night-time struggle I had told myself that I had done enough 'what is good'. I mustn't think that I had to do everything. I already worked with OM, had lots of young people in the home, lived without a salary, had adopted a child already. Was this not enough? The Lord took that argument out of my hands that morning. It wasn't enough! I was only thirty-three years old. I still had my whole life ahead of me to devote myself to doing good works and to continue to show his love in that way.

When I read the passage that morning, I already knew God's answer, but I had also asked for one thousand guilders and I wanted to stick to that. During breakfast I shared my feelings with Kees and the children, and together we prayed for the confirmation of one thousand guilders. Kees left for the office and returned ten minutes later. With the post there was a letter from a girl who hadn't written to us in years and who now suddenly sent six hundred guilders for 'something special in your family'. I could hardly believe it! First the Bible verse that had touched me deeply and now, so quickly, already six hundred guilders from someone who didn't know our situation. If I had stuck to my first target of five hundred guilders, the prayer would already have been answered. But I had asked for one thousand.

On Wednesday, Thursday and Friday nothing happened. No money, no letters and no cheques. It now became exciting. Everything pointed to God confirming our desires. On the Friday evening the OM team from Zaventem joined our team for a time of prayer. It sometimes happened that some of our post was sent to Zaventem. That evening they brought along a whole pile of letters. While the others prayed, we opened our post. There was money in just about every letter. We received dollars, pounds, Swiss francs and Swedish Krones. It was all meant 'for the family'. We had much more than one thousand guilders!

Needless to say we immediately posted the adoption papers that Saturday morning. God had answered us by giving us what we had asked of him and by confirming to us through his Word that this was his will for our lives and to 'stress these things' and to do 'what is good'. Four and a half months later, Karin arrived. She was three and a half years old, happy and easy-going. She came through the door, and made herself right at home. It was as if she had always been there. The Lord had a plan with her life and with our family and he did his utmost to make this clear to us.

Perhaps I can mention here that during the months before and many months after this incident we never received one extra gift. Everything came in that one week. The Bible verse the Lord used was left in its context. Through it God gave us a message that was necessary at that time, but we can also apply it for the rest of our lives and for the lives of all other people who put their trust in God. Of course, the verse does not mean that everybody has to adopt children, but it does mean that all Christians should be first in doing good.

Recently, the Lord touched me again very specifically through his Word. We went through great problems with our work. Everything we had built through the years seemed to be crumbling. I was very discouraged and the future seemed one big, insecure and dark hole. One day I couldn't move from my bed. I just lay there crying. Kees had gone to a conference, the children were in school and emotionally I was drained. Around half past ten the phone rang and after a disconsolate conversation with a friend, I took up my Bible study diary and with a

cry in my heart I said: 'Lord, what must I do?' The Bible
verses for that day were striking. They said: 'Wait, my
daughter...Keep calm and don't be afraid. Do not lose
heart...Be still, and know that I am God' (Ruth 3:18;
Isaiah 7:4; Psalm 46:10). The message was clear and
agreed with the teachings of the whole Bible. I had to
cease being so nervous and discouraged. I had to put the
whole situation, which I couldn't change anyway, into
the hands of God and trust him. I dried away my tears,
got up out of bed and made myself a good cup of coffee.
I faced the rest of the day with hope, knowing that God
would take care of us. His Word had spoken to me in a
special way when I was down and made clear to me what
I had to do: be quiet, wait and trust.

2. Through prayer. 'If any of you lacks wisdom, he
should ask God, who gives generously to all without
finding fault; and it will be given to him' (James 1:5).
God wants us to pray about everything! It is wonderful
that God simply gives in this way without finding fault.
In both the situations that I have just told you about,
God had the right to reproach my unbelief and doubt.
After all, I had been living with the Lord for twenty-six
years, I had taught others about these things, written
about them and preached about them. When, in spite of
everything, I cried out to the Lord in great discourage-
ment and said: 'Lord what shall I do?', he answered
without any reproach. That is our God!

Sometimes guidance from above does not come
immediately. Paul writes to the Thessalonians that he
prays fervently day and night in order that God will give
him the opportunity to come to them. Paul also encourages us to pray without ceasing. God answers our
prayers about his guidance. Sometimes the answers
come immediately. Sometimes he wants us to persevere

in prayer. One thing is for sure! God wants to guide us
and he wants us to pray for it!

3. Through the Holy Spirit. God gave us his Spirit in
order to lead us from within. This is one of the big
differences between God's guidance today and God's
guidance under the old covenant. God's Spirit, living in
us, wants to guide us and make God's will known to us.
The apostles even dared to write in their letter to the
Christians in Antioch: 'It seemed good to the Holy Spirit
and to us' (Acts 15:28). This tells us of a tremendous
confidence in a sure knowledge of God's will! Our conviction with regard to the guidance of God's Spirit in our
lives of course always has to be tested on God's Word,
God's confirmation and also on the conviction of fellow-
Christians. It is certain that all those led through God's
Spirit must first be children of God and that the Holy
Spirit is given to us to lead us into all truth.

4. Through the advice of friends. Proverbs tells us to
listen to advice of our brothers and sisters in Christ. 'But
a wise man listens to advice' (Proverbs 12:15); 'But with
many advisers they succeed' (Proverbs 15:22); 'For victory [you need] many advisers' (Proverbs 24:6). The
apostles in Acts 15 talked about the Holy Spirit and us!
They had discussed the issue thoroughly, and had looked
at it from all sides. It is clear from this chapter that some
of them didn't agree at all. But through the discussions,
which might have been quite heated from time to time,
they came to the same conclusion that this was the will of
the Holy Spirit. When God saved us, he did not intend
us to live a life of a hermit. He gave each of us the Holy
Spirit within, but also placed us together in one Body.
He even emphasises that this universal Body, which can
sound quite abstract, is not the only thing that unites us.
He doesn't want us to miss the local meetings of

believers, even with all their faults and limitations. The purpose of it all is surely that we can support and comfort one another, but also encourage and correct each other. As an individual it is easy to get side-tracked, you can start seeing things in a totally different light. Together with the brothers and sisters who have also received the Holy Spirit and who know you with all your weaknesses and strengths, there is a bigger chance of understanding God's guidance and of making the right decisions.

5. *Through God's confirmation.* Just as God gave to Abraham's servant a wonderful confirmation which led him to make the right choice, he also wants to confirm the important decisions in our life in this special way. David often prays that God will confirm his way. As with Abraham's servant, as with Gideon, and as in our case with the adoption, God sometimes does this in a strange way. Looking back at my twenty-six years of being a Christian, I must admit it hasn't happened to me all that often. It's also not a common occurrence in the Bible. In most cases God confirms something in your life through his Holy Spirit, his Word, the advice of others and through circumstances. Paul speaks about an 'open door' (1 Corinthians 16:8, 9) from which he concludes that God was leading him to stay in Ephesus during Pentecost.

When I look back on our years of 'Christian work' and the decisions we had to make, I have to say that God has guided us most of the time through circumstances. When we finished Bible college we never heard a voice from heaven telling us to go to Halle. During the summer an evangelistic outreach took place there and afterwards there was the need for a young couple to do follow-up. We were asked to consider this. The 'open door' was to us the most important indication of God's guidance. When we were asked later to lead the OM work in

Belgium and the Netherlands, we saw God's hand in that. We were also attracted to the way OM worked and operated (confirmation of the Holy Spirit in our hearts). We chose Louvain as our base since this famous university city with its twenty-five thousand students challenged us to do student work. Looking back, we can honestly say that the Lord clearly guided us in these decisions, and yet, it was nothing spectacular.

6. *Through God's hindrance.* Sometimes God opens the door on our way, but he can also stop us continuing what we are doing. In Acts 16 we see that Paul is on one of his journeys and everything is going well. The churches are confirmed in their faith through his ministry and people are coming to the Lord. You would tend to say that he should continue doing so. But then something odd happens. The Holy Spirit keeps them from preaching the word in Asia (Acts 16:6). Afterwards they try to travel to Bithynia, but the Spirit of Jesus would not allow them to, so they continue to Mysia and Troas. In Troas Paul receives the vision to come to Macedonia. Immediately they look for the opportunity to go to Macedonia, while they become convinced that through all this God is calling them to preach the gospel there. Indeed, they find in Philippi the woman Lydia, a dealer in purple cloth, who becomes converted and afterwards many wonderful things take place in this area of Europe.

Is this not interesting and encouraging? Generally, Paul and his team simply follow the map. They travel from town to town and God lets them do that. But when God has another plan for them, he prevents them from continuing and very clearly shows them what the following step must be. This is a great encouragement to all of us. Let's continue to grow in our dependency on God, and do the things that are most logical. If God has another plan for us it will become clear to us.

Twice Kees and I have tried to go to work in India, and twice God prevented us going in such a way that we could not deny it. From these clear hindrances we concluded that God wanted us to stay in Belgium. These things have strengthened my confidence that I don't have to be scared or uptight in my decisions. When my daily attitude in life is one of dependency on God, then God will direct my life. He has many ways of stopping us if he wants to.

7. Through God's sovereign intervention. Everything in our life can sometimes change through some dramatic happening, like having a handicapped child, suffering from cancer or being wounded so badly that we are paralysed. All these things we can only place in the category of God's divine intervention in our life. Only God knows the 'why' of these things in which we have no say. Acceptance and letting God continue his work through our weakness is all that is left to us. God sometimes has a completely different plan for the rest of our lives than we had thought or wished for. Sometimes, as in Job's case, it is a divine test of our love and trust in him. We could later discover that it was preparation for a completely different and difficult task for which maturity and experience was needed, as in Joseph's case. In many cases we will never know the reason why, but that our life drastically changes through such events is quite clear.

If our lives belong to God and if we want to follow him and serve him with the gifts he has given us, then it is very important to learn to distinguish the will of God in our lives. Life can be a joy when you know he leads you. It saves you so much worry, so much sorrow and feelings of guilt when life becomes difficult. The knowledge that God is with you, and that his secure and faithful hand is leading you, is one of the most precious things a human being can experience. He is our loving, abundantly giving Father. So we can leave behind any feelings of fear and insecurity with regard to these things and continue on our way in full confidence, hand in hand with Jesus.

6

I Can't Forgive!

How difficult it can be to forgive! How mean people can be! How easily we can feel hurt! As a normal human being, how can you be expected just to forgive? It is fully understandable that we keep thinking about it. After all, how can you allow people to just walk over you?

Do you know this line of thought? Well, you're not the only one. Peter had the same problem. With his hot-headed personality he felt that to forgive seven times was quite an achievement, and I must say that I quite agree with him. But Jesus had a different opinion about this very human problem and he tried to explain this to Peter (and to us) with the following story.

Once upon a time there was a king who wanted to settle accounts with his slaves. One of the slaves was not doing too well financially. He owed his lord over a hundred thousand pounds. This was a phenomenal amount to him, more than one person would be able to earn in his whole life. An awful debt, a hopeless situation! When the person in question humbled himself before his lord in his deep, deep misery and begged for mercy for himself and his family, the lord took pity and wrote it off as bad debt.

Great! You would expect the poor man to go home jumping with joy and thankfulness to inform his wife of these good tidings. But no, things went differently. On his way home he met somebody who owed him a few pounds. He seized the man's collar and insisted that he should repay the money immediately. The poor fellow had nothing and could not pay. The first man, who had just been freed of a great debt, then proceeded to put his debtor in prison for just a few pounds (Matthew 18:21–35).

I am sure the Lord had a very good reason for using two such ridiculous amounts. The one amount ridiculously high, unpayable! The other amount ridiculously low, negligible. The meaning of the story is clear. God's forgiveness to us is great and overwhelming. The message of the New as well as the Old Testament is: 'He will freely pardon' (Isaiah 55:7). All our unrighteousness, all our sins and failures have been put away by him. Thankfulness, joy and an attitude of generous forgiving towards the people around us should be the normal reaction of our hearts!

But most times it is not the case. If somebody has offended us, we spend many sleepless nights thinking about it. If somebody said something bad about us behind our backs, we are very quick to respond in a nasty way. Even though the Lord forgave us our huge debts, we keep presenting the few pounds that someone else owes us, day after day. The Bible however warns us that we cannot continue doing this and remain unpunished. If we refuse to forgive other people, there will be spiritual, emotional and physical consequences.

The cost of unforgiveness

If we don't learn to forgive, we can expect serious spiritual consequences. Even though God is full of love, mercy and forgiveness, he warns us in the Bible time and time again about the consequences of our lack of forgiveness. The end of the story in Matthew 18 is not that the man who couldn't pay the few pounds spent the rest of his life in prison, but that the king was furious with the man who had received so much forgiveness, but who in turn could not forgive the other person. The Lord Jesus then ends his story with a warning to Peter, the other disciples and to us with: 'This is how my heavenly Father will treat each of you unless you forgive your brother from your heart' (Matthew 18:35).

This is not the only occasion when the Lord Jesus speaks about these things. In Matthew 6 we find, in the 'Lord's Prayer', that the Lord links the forgiveness of our sins to the forgiveness we grant others (verse 12). In verse 14 of the same chapter, when he finishes his prayer, the Lord underlines this one aspect for which he prayed. He does not remind us once more to pray for our daily bread—he knows very well that when we get hungry, we will pray for that. No, he emphasises once more the matter we find so difficult, and says: 'For if you forgive men when they sin against you, your heavenly Father will also forgive you. But if you do not forgive men their sins, your Father will not forgive your sins!' (Matthew 6:14,15).

When we seriously consider this, we come to the conclusion that it is one of the simplest commands in the Bible, but despite all of our Christian upbringing and theological teachings, we trample it underfoot. Still, this is not something we can just put aside. It is a command! Paul says: 'Bear with each other and forgive whatever grievances you may have against one another. Forgive as the Lord forgave you!' (Colossians 3:13).

Here again we see the connection between God's forgiveness towards us and our forgiveness towards others. The first, and possibly the most serious spiritual consequence, is that if we cannot forgive others, there is just no way that God can forgive us.

Together with this we read in Mark 11:24,25 that our prayers will not be answered if we bear unforgiveness in our hearts. Our whole attitude towards God and our free communication with him will be dimmed by our disobedience if we live with feelings of resentment and unforgiveness.

The serious emotional consequences of unforgiveness

If somebody really hurts us, we will be angry. Some people are more easily offended than others. Some people are easily angered and offended by little things. You might discover that one of your friends who was away on holiday sent postcards to others, but not to you. Maybe there was a birthday party and several of your friends were invited, but not you. Or it could be more serious. Somebody blasted you in public and you feel humiliated and angry. Worse is when they have slandered you behind your back. You were not there. You couldn't say anything in your defence. Almost everybody would be hurt and angry about this sort of thing. One of the worst things that can happen in life is perhaps to discover that the partner you love has deceived you and run off with somebody else. All your self-confidence and self-worth is affected by this and you are hurting.

There are many ways in which people can emotionally hurt us. It is quite normal and human that we are offended and angry about such things. To become angry is in itself a 'normal' reaction of our wounded emotions and I don't think this is always wrong. In the Old Testament we quite often see that God becomes angry with people, with nations and even with his own people. Also, in the New Testament, we see how the Lord Jesus gets angry. In Mark 3:5 the Lord becomes angry with the Jews about hardening their hearts and their legal and unmerciful attitude with regard to men in need.

There is therefore a justified anger, an emotional reaction towards unjustified things. But if we remain angry, feed and work up our anger, then it becomes sin. In Ephesians 4:26 Paul says: 'Do not let the sun go down while you are still angry, and do not give the devil a foothold.' In other words: if you have been hurt and you become angry—this can happen and it does not have to be sin. But if you *stay* angry and do not forgive before the end of the day, then something is fundamentally wrong and you are moving into the devil's territory.

If we do not forgive quickly, we remain angry. Anger causes resentment and bitterness, both things the Bible judges (Ephesians 4:31, Hebrews 12:15), and also things that have a deep and terrible influence on our feelings. A person who entertains feelings of resentment is never happy or relaxed. He cannot enjoy the good things because everything is overshadowed by his resentment and bitterness. Bitter people have a bad effect on others, but an even worse effect on themselves. Hebrews 12:15 warns us against this bitterness which causes confusion and by which many are defiled.

We see this all around us. Nothing is as contagious as bitterness. A conflict between two people in a church that is not forgiven and resolved, all too often results in the bitterness defiling many others and even in a split in the church. Bitter people are hostile and extremely critical. They distrust everything and everyone. Sometimes they use revenge to give expression to their bitterness in that way. The Bible is also very clear on these matters.

'Do not repay anyone evil for evil. Be careful to do what is right in the eyes of everybody. If it is possible, as far as it depends on you, live at peace with everyone. Do not take revenge, my friends, but leave room for God's wrath, for it is written: "It is mine to avenge; I will repay," says the Lord. On the contrary: "If your enemy is hungry, feed him; if he is thirsty, give him something to drink. In doing this, you will heap burning coals on his head." Do not be overcome by evil, but overcome evil with good' (Romans 12:17–21).

Another result of hostility and bitterness can be that we become depressed. All joy and peace will be removed from our lives and the emotional consequences will be enormous for ourselves and for all those around us. A few years ago I heard the testimony of a woman who had a serious conflict with someone during her youth. The person involved had hurt her by sending her a very nasty letter, and for thirty years this woman saved that letter in her cupboard. If she, in a conversation, heard something good about her 'enemy' she would take out the letter and read it again. Automatically her hatred and hostility welled up inside her once more.

But then she met Christ. Gradually, while studying the Bible, she started to realise that she had to destroy the letter and forgive the other person. This resulted in an emotional battle within her. That letter had become a part of her, and was the symbol of her hatred and resentment. But she understood that there was no choice. Her own Christian life depended upon destroying this letter. In the end she burned it. It was as if, at the same time as the destruction of the letter, a terrible weight was lifted from her. She told her husband and also phoned the other person to ask her forgiveness. The next Sunday she confessed what she had done in tears to the church. The breakthrough had come in her life.

Unforgiveness can even have physical consequences

The enormous emotional stresses that are awakened by hate and resentment can definitely have an effect on our bodies. The first physical result of not having forgiven before the sun goes down after somebody has hurt you is that you cannot sleep! The situation replays itself in your mind all the time, and your anger increases. You toss and turn in your bed. Eventually you end up with a headache and the next morning you will feel even more miserable! The only way to prevent yourself from experiencing such a bad night is simply to forgive the other person before the sun goes down.

When you allow the situation to carry on longer than it should, you lose your joy, you become tired, and as the weeks go by and the whole matter is not forgiven, there will be more and more physical complaints. You might experience more frequent headaches. Others, who have weak stomachs, may end up with chronic stomachaches or stomach ulcers. Other people might get backaches or problems with high blood pressure. The ongoing stress can in some cases even lead to a heart attack.

Of course I do not wish to suggest that all people suffering from these sorts of complaints got them because they did not forgive. There can be many causes for these complaints. But we must understand that hatred, bitterness and unforgiveness can in the long run have an important bearing on health. Some people, by nature, forgive much more easily than others. Some people set very high standards for themselves and expect the same from others. Other people suffer from inferiority complexes and are thus easily offended and wounded. Others can brush any offence aside. But sooner or later each one of us will have to forgive something that, to us, will seem really difficult.

This subject is one that I have studied and often spoken about. A few years ago, I really felt that the subject of forgiveness was something that I had understood well and that the Lord had put upon my heart. But the next year, many things started happening which I found very hard and difficult to understand. For the first time in my life I discovered that to forgive wasn't as easy as I had thought. I wrestled with my feelings, lying awake at night, but every time I decided that now it must be over and I must forgive and forget the matter, something happened that brought everything back again.

One evening I got terrible stomach pains. They were so bad that I was rolling around in bed. Kees came to me and said: 'Toos, you will have to surrender your feelings and hurt to the Lord, because I am afraid this is giving you stomach ulcers.' That made me even more scared!

The pain became so acute that I had to go into hospital the next day. Well, to cut a long story short, it was not an ulcer, but a pregnancy outside the womb which had burst my fallopian tube and had caused inner bleeding. I was immediately operated on and everything went well. The people who had caused me such difficulty were the first to come and visit me. They showered me with flowers, attention and love.

During the weeks in the hospital and later at home, I had lots of time to be still and to think. God had the chance to remove all of my bitterness and confusion. It was a time of spiritual breakthrough, and was certainly a very beneficial experience!

One year later things happened that were a hundred times worse. We felt betrayed by the people whom we had trusted completely. Criticism and gossip was the order of the day. It was the most difficult time in our lives. I will not say that we found it easy to cope with. But there was a fundamental difference from the conflict of the year before; I did not find it difficult to forgive. I was able to forgive the people who had caused us so much pain. This was the result of the work God had done in my life the year before.

Do I find forgiving easier now? No! Every time we encounter injustice, we become angry. That is a human reaction. But the command of the Lord is very clear. Through the practical steps of forgiving we will get to know a new way of life; the kind of life the Lord Jesus led; the kind of life that forgives.

To forgive is a matter of the will

In our day and age and in our West European culture, our emotions play an important part in our decisions. The Bible, however, attaches more importance to action than to our feelings about it. The important aspect in the matter of forgiveness is not my feelings with regard to these people, but the fact that God says I have to forgive them. A decision of the will, even if it runs contrary to all my feelings, is the first step to forgiveness.

1. Honest confrontation. In Leviticus 19:17 God instructs the Jews: 'Do not hate your brother in your heart. Rebuke your neighbour frankly so that you will not share in his guilt.'

This is an extremely important step in the whole process of forgiveness. It is not easy, but very beneficial, to have an honest talk with the person concerned if you have been hurt.

Following a lengthy period of disunity on our team, I discovered that the wives on the team wrestled much more with feelings of resentment than did the men. This surprised me and I looked into the cause of it. Gradually it became clear to me that the disunity and conflicts were originally among the men and all work-related. The wives, who spent most of their time in their own homes, would often hear things from their husbands, and be bothered by them. The men, however, met again at work the next day, and usually sorted out their problems. For more serious conflicts the men would all meet together and discuss their differences of opinion. Usually they came to some kind of reconciliation.

But the women never got to hear the other people's

point of view, and could never express the way they felt. This led to a continuous feeling of frustration and eventually of resentment.

2. Put Christian principles into practice. Christ, who met only with injustice and misunderstanding in his life, had a forgiving way of living! Time and time again he approached people with these words: 'Your sins are forgiven.'

This same Christ lives in us! If we give him the chance and the space, then his disposition of forgiveness will become ours. The Holy Spirit, who dwells in us, will also do his work in us. The fruit of the Spirit is, among other things, patience, kindness and self-control, all things which are connected with forgiveness.

If everything within you cries out in anger, resentment and bitterness, read the most important Bible portions about forgiveness, memorise them and hang them on your wall! They will certainly have an effect on your life!

3. Control your mind. This is a major battlefield. Philippians 4:8 urges us to think only those things which are right, pure, lovely, praiseworthy and excellent.

Every time the memories of what has happened come back to us, we have to check ourselves immediately and direct our minds towards that which is positive. I admit that this is no easy thing, but we can invent ways to achieve it. When I wake up in the middle of the night, it does sometimes happen that waves of memories come back to me. Instead of giving in to them and allowing myself to get angry or sad again, I now take action. I get up, take my Bible or a book and put my mind by force onto positive things. After some time I can go back to bed, blessed by what I have read and finding that the memories have gone. If we conquer our minds, we are well on our way to conquering our problem of not being able to forgive.

4. *Learn to understand the other person.* When we have been hurt by someone, it is often very difficult to understand the background, character and situation of the 'wrong-doer'. I can assure you that it helps to overcome your anger, bitterness, resentment by getting to know more about the other person.

One of our team members who was normally quite jovial and friendly, suddenly underwent a change in attitude. He lost his motivation to work and became very unreasonable and irritable. When we discovered what he was going through at home, we could understand his behaviour. He and his wife had a new baby who was crying all night, and his wife had been ill with a high fever ever since coming home from hospital. Not surprisingly this had affected his whole attitude. Instead of being angry, we were then able to be concerned and tried to help him.

Above all, recognise again and again your own failure in many areas and the forgiveness you yourself need daily.

5. *Don't state conditions.* Often we are quite ready to forgive when the other party comes to us to ask for forgiveness and when he seems to have learned his lesson. This is, however, not a condition for forgiveness. We are responsible to God for keeping our hearts clean of all resentment and bitterness. The other person is responsible to God for his heart, his confession of guilt and his forgiveness with regard to me.

6. *Keep your eye on the eternal perspective!* Joseph is a wonderful example. He suffered so much injustice and hardship at the hands of his own brothers. They hated

him and were horrible to him. But, in Genesis 45:5–9, Joseph says to his brothers, 'It was to save lives that God sent me ahead of you.'

This is so contrary to what we are used to. His brothers had thrown him into a pit and sold him as a slave. But Joseph's heart knew no bitterness. He saw God's sovereign hand upon his life, even in the meanness of his brothers. That's why he could forgive wholeheartedly and return good for evil. In Genesis 50, when their father Jacob has died, the brothers become nervous again. Their conscience accuses them and they are afraid that Joseph will take revenge. When Joseph hears about this, it hurts him so much that he starts to cry. He holds nothing against his brothers! He loves them and wants to help them. Drying his tears, he calls out to them: 'Don't be afraid. Am I in the place of God? You intended to harm me, but God intended it for good to accomplish what is now being done, the saving of many lives' (Genesis 50:19–21).

What an example of how it can and should be! I am convinced that Joseph practised this attitude of forgiveness from a very early age. Let us, just like Joseph, train ourselves in seeing God's perspective in the little things in our lives. Our hearts and emotions will then react in the proper way when the big test comes.

7. *Express your forgiveness in words.* Always express your forgiveness verbally. If the person concerned knows that you are having problems with him, speak your forgiveness directly to him. If he is not aware of any problems, talk to a minister or trusted friend instead. If you have mentioned your feelings of resentment to someone else, don't forget to go back and say that you have now forgiven.

If you feel that you cannot speak about the offence to anyone, then take it to the Lord. In prayer, tell the Lord that you have sincerely forgiven the person who hurt you. I remember a time when difficult things had taken place in our church and I was extremely upset and angry with some of the people. My husband was on a journey and the matters were too serious to share them with the children. I had no one to talk with! The problem of my anger was even more pressing because of the fact that I had to speak that weekend at a women's retreat about the subject of—forgiving!

One evening I nearly exploded with anger and I decided to do something about it. I put on my track-suit and ran all the way to the forest in order to get rid of some of my aggression. In the woods I told the Lord out loud how angry I was. I even mentioned the names of the people involved and promised the Lord to forgive them, though my emotions were still running high. This action of the will was all I could do at that point. Yet God knew my willingness to obey. A certain peace settled in my heart again. I did not find it easy to speak on forgiveness that weekend but did it anyway, knowing that I had promised God to forgive.

I am convinced that if we start practising these things, we will develop a way of living in which we will be able to forgive. What encourages me constantly, is that the Bible speaks about forgiving 'whole-heartedly'. It is not a mean, niggling way of doing things, in which we grudgingly promise to overlook something. No, it is whole-hearted and abundant, just like God's forgiveness is abundant. Proverbs 19:11 says: 'A man's wisdom gives him patience; it is to his glory to overlook an offence.'

7

Help, I'm Scared!

Sometimes we openly admit that we are scared, but more often we just deny it. From a young age we become quite specialised in manoeuvring ourselves into such a position that we don't have to do that which we fear most. Fear plays a big role in the life of many people, even if they would not like to admit it. For a Christian the situation is even more difficult. When you have found true faith in the almighty God and begun to trust him who leads and guides all things in life, then there should be no reason to be afraid. To admit that you are scared sounds terribly unspiritual and that's why we don't say it. Still, it appears that many Christians are imprisoned by their fears.

What is fear?

Fear is a normal and necessary emotion. In a life full of danger, we need fear to protect us. For example, it is very useful that we are scared when a car is heading towards us at full speed. The fear inspires us and gets the adrenalin pumping—so we are able to jump aside and live on to fight another day. It's also good to be afraid of fire. A young toddler who has not yet developed this fear has to be watched carefully. Fear for heights helps us not to go close to the edge of the ravine, and not to hang too far out of the window. Fear in itself is not wrong or unspiritual, but a normal emotion.

Even though fear is a useful and normal emotion— even though it is a part of the weaknesses of human life and doesn't need to be a sin—fear can still start to control us and become the determining factor in our lives. In that case, something is wrong somewhere. God doesn't want us to be imprisoned by fear, which is one of the reasons why Jesus came into this world to 'destroy him who holds the power of death—that is, the devil— and free those who all their lives were held in slavery by their fear of death' (Hebrews 2:14,15).

What does the Bible say about fear?

Even though we are usually ashamed about our fears and try to pretend to be more courageous than we really are, we see an open confession of fear in the Bible. David absolutely excels in describing his fear:

> 'Fear and trembling have beset me;
> horror has overwhelmed me' (Psalm 55:5).

This description doesn't leave any doubt about David's emotional state at the time. It is important to be honest about your fears and, as we will see later on, honesty is the first step to victory.

But this is not all that we find in the Bible about fear. Most of the relevant passages serve as a means of encouraging us not to be afraid. God knows that, by nature, we are fearful people, but time and again he challenges us not to be afraid. For example, in Joshua 1, we read four times in succession God's command and challenge to young Joshua, who is going to take on a new command. God's words are: 'Be strong and courageous' (verse 6); 'Be strong and very courageous' (verse 7); 'Have I not commanded you? Be strong and courageous. Do not be terrified; do not be discouraged, for the Lord your God will be with you wherever you go' (verse 9). At the end he says once more: 'Only be strong and coura- geous!' (verse 18). The message is clear and not to be misunderstood. God knows that it will not be easy for Joshua. God knows the human heart that is full of fear and uncertainties. That's why he continually encourages us to be strong and courageous.

The basis for these exhortations is not the fact that we will somehow manage or that things are probably not as bad as we think, but that we are in God's power and presence. In Isaiah 41:10 he says to his people: 'So do not fear, for I am with you; do not be dismayed, for I am your God. I will strengthen you and help you; I will uphold you with my righteous right hand.' When we look at the New Testament we see that God's message is the same: 'Fear not!' These are God's first words when the angel appears to Zechariah, to Mary and to the shep- herds. God knows that our first reaction is one of fear and that's why he starts by reassuring us. The Lord Jesus himself encourages his disciples again and again with the words: 'Do not be afraid.' After the resurrection there is the same message: 'Do not be afraid. Go and tell my brothers...' (Matthew 28:10).

To our surprise we see that even the apostle Paul, a man who went through so much for the sake of the gospel, needed this encouragement from time to time. Twice we find Paul having to put aside his fear and speak, despite his difficult situation. The reassuring words 'For I am with you' are added to it. We can come to the conclusion that Paul, in spite of the fact that he was a courageous man, also dreaded certain things and knew fear. Paul, in his turn, encourages Timothy to be strong and he underlines this by reminding his young friend that he had not received 'a spirit of timidity, but a spirit of power...' (2 Timothy 1:7).

The risen Lord, who was taken up to heaven, greets his beloved disciple John in the Revelation with the words: 'Do not be afraid. I am the First and the Last' (Revelation 1:17).

The last verse about this subject in the Bible is possibly also the most difficult one. A verse that makes us shrink back and say: 'No, Lord, I can't do that.' In Revelation 2:10 Jesus says to his church: 'Do not be afraid of what you are about to suffer.' He adds that some will be put into prison and that there will be tribulation. No promises of only roses and rapture, but the command: 'Be faithful, even to the point of death, and I will give you the crown of life.'

The Lord knows our heart, and therefore the misery of fear is quite regularly described in the Bible. But it is not the determining factor. God challenges his children not to be afraid and to put their trust in him, even if things are bad and even if trusting him means death. It is very important to understand this message of the Bible. Some Christians interpret their feelings of fear as something of 'God's leading' that they shouldn't do a particular thing. They will say: 'I don't have peace about it' or something similar. Actually they mean that they are scared. A healthy self-criticism is quite important in these matters. Am I really convinced of the fact that this is not God's will or am I simply afraid? And if I am simply afraid, how do I find the courage to do what I have to do?

Steps to overcoming fear

1. Honestly recognise your fear. This is not easy for us. I have wrestled with many fears. It's natural that some are more easily scared than others. As a child and young girl

I was very scared to be left at home alone. We lived above a tailor's shop, and when it was dark, I was really scared of these dark rooms downstairs, full of shadows, rows of clothes, cupboards and boxes.

My fears came to a climax during the years we were newly married. We lived alone, again in an old, creaking house, and when it got dark, I was very aware of our lonely country road. Kees was away most evenings. He was then the pastor of a small evangelical church in Belgium and in the evening he visited people, led Bible studies and prayer meetings. Then other fears began to grow. I was very afraid of losing my husband in a traffic accident, or losing my children. As a young, pregnant woman and later as a mother of small children you feel very vulnerable!

Fear in the car! There was no way I dared to learn to drive the car myself, until Kees persuaded me to do it. But one fear dominated the rest. My fear of flying! When my husband started to work more on an international level and started flying more often, my fear developed into a really acute problem. When two of my friends died in different plane crashes in the same year, I swore that I would never ever put a foot in an aeroplane.

My sister and brother-in-law had meanwhile left the country to work as doctors in the Middle East. Kees had visited them twice and time and time again he urged me to pay them a visit. I trembled at the mere thought of it and comforted myself that we didn't have the money for it anyway and as a mother of four children there was no way I could go.

But then, out of the blue, I received the money to visit my sister and Kees offered to look after the children! Robbed of all excuses I was forced to say I would go. For months on end I had sleepless nights and used valium to keep something of a grip on myself. When I read about a plane crash in the newspaper I immediately started crying. Kees was of course well aware of my fears but remained insistent that I should go. He both encouraged and teased me and did not forget to mention that there was a slight chance of me coming back safely. But I could not imagine coming back home in one piece and got him to promise that he would find a good mother for our kids.

By this time loads of people had heard that I was going to visit my sister, and time after time they would say; 'How nice for you, Toos, that you can visit your sister. I am sure you are looking forward to it!' I would simply smile bravely and nod happily but inwardly I would be thinking: 'If only they knew!' I would have given anything not to go.

On the other hand, I was still portraying the image of a strong woman. I was leading meetings, spoke regularly at conferences and did all those things easily which for other women are frightening.

One evening I had been to a meeting with a friend of mine. I will never forget that evening. With the rain pouring down, we were driving home when suddenly my friend said to me: 'Isn't it wonderful, Toos, that you can go and visit your sister!' Suddenly it all became too much for me. I burst into tears, pulled the car in by the side of the road and poured out my fears. My friend did not know what had hit her! We then talked for a long time and prayed together about this fear of mine. Even though this time of prayer did not take away my fears, it was still a tremendous emotional relief to be able to talk about it and to pray with someone. The following week we had a meeting with all the women on our team and there again I took the difficult step of sharing my fear and asking them to pray for me.

This honest recognition of my fear, and asking for prayer in all humility, was the first big step on the way to liberty. James 5:16 says that we should confess our sins and pray for one another in order to receive healing. If this is the case with sin, then it is surely the case with our weaknesses.

I have to add that I was not immediately free of my fear. When I went on my trip I was still very scared. To my surprise I returned safely to Belgium. My fear of flying was still not totally gone, but I did realise that all the good things I experienced on that trip far outweighed my misery and fear. When I came back I made a decision that I would never again refrain from doing something just because of fear.

2. Train yourself in faith and trust. In Psalm 56:3,4 we read: 'When I am afraid, I will trust in you. In God, whose word I praise, in God I trust; I will not be afraid. What can mortal man do to me?'

This verse shows us a wonderful change in David's emotional life. He starts with fear and with this fear he goes to God in whom he trusts. And then there is the change. Then trust gets the upper hand and his fear resolves. He then also sees what man could do to him in its true perspectives. It is good to recognise your fears and admit it to yourself and before others, but don't leave it at that! You will never overcome the fear of a particular thing if you don't step out in faith and do it.

I would never have overcome my fear of flying if I had refused to step into an aeroplane. When, later on, Kees and I made a long journey through Africa and we had to transfer from one plane to the next, in good weather and in bad weather, in big jumbo jets and in small one-engine planes, I had to use all the determination I had in order to trust God with my fear. Slowly but surely I discovered that my trust grew and my heart started to beat slower when we took off, until I honestly could say: 'In God I trust, I fear not!' That was a wonderful feeling and moment, the moment I realised that my fear was gone! It is a deliverance, a victory! I never experienced that fear again. I rather enjoy flying now. Trusting in God totally in this way plays a major part in overcoming fear. It has to do with letting go of everything you are holding on to.

Often the basis of it all is our fear of dying. Our fear for flying and driving, fear of hospitals and operations, all comes down to our fear of dying. Our fears also multiply when we get married and have children. Now we are fearful that something terrible would happen to our husbands or children. We suddenly have so many more lives for which to fear.

Only when we learn to put our lives, and the lives of those we love, into God's hand and train ourselves in that respect, will this destructive fear loosen its grip. When I found myself in the midst of this learning process and wrestled with my fears, we received an invitation to speak at a conference in Eastern Europe. My conversations with the Christians there, hearing about the enormous risks they take every day, helped me to overcome my fear. I started to realise that they were people just like us. They were not holier or by nature more courageous. But they had, because of their circumstances, let go of the everyday fears which were binding them. When we heard about one plan of theirs, our response was one of utter amazement. 'But that's too dangerous,' we said. 'We are not afraid of the risks when we know the reward is worth the trouble,' they laughed. I was reminded of the attitude of Queen Esther: 'If I die, I die.'

Brother Andrew, one of the first to make known the plight of our brothers and sisters in Eastern Europe, said; 'A hero is someone who is scared, but still gets the job done!'

If you are willing, in principle, to decide to let go of those things over which you have basically no power anyway, you will discover that this will release your fears. The Lord Jesus himself urges us to that line of action in Luke 12: 'Who of you by worrying can add a single hour to his life? Since you cannot do this very little thing, why do you worry about the rest?' (verses 25,26).

We know these words by heart, but it is so difficult to put them into practice. The only way to start is by doing exactly that which you fear most. Put your foot upon the waters, give your life with your shaking knees into God's hands and start doing that which you wouldn't normally dare to do.

When I started to do things of which I was deadly afraid and God's grace started to grow in me and my fear diminished, I discovered that this had many effects. Not only did I lose my one fear, but slowly but surely my other fears disappeared as well. Another result was that I started to sleep much better. For years I had used sleeping tablets regularly. When my fears diminished and my trust grew, a healthy sleep returned. Reluctantly I had let go of something only to discover that I was set free of the fears that had kept me in bondage.

3. Always put your obedience to God above your fear. There is no way you can see your fear as a spiritual indication to refrain from doing a certain thing or taking a particular line of action.

Jesus did the will of his Father despite the knowledge of the suffering he was to endure. 'He learned obedience from what he suffered' (Hebrews 5:8). Queen Esther was also aware of the risks she was taking. She asked all Jews to fast and pray with her and her servants for three days and three nights. After that she went to the king, in spite of the penalty such an action carried. She knew what the consequences could be. She knew the penalty was death! But she was driven by something greater. If she didn't take the risk all of her people would die.

Despite her fears, she realised and recognised her responsibility before God and her people. What a terrible dilemma for this young woman! She placed her obedience to God above her fear, and then did what she knew was right. God honoured that. He rewarded her courage and saved her and her people (Esther 4).

'But even if he does not...' (Daniel 3:18) cried four young men in an even more precarious position! 'But even if he does not, we want you to know, O king, that we will not serve your gods or worship the image of gold you have set up.' Daniel and his friends knew that their first priority was obedience to God—unconditionally. They needed readiness and willingness to meet the challenges head-on, in spite of the prospect of physical suffering and even death.

How do you attain this? Simply by being faithful and obedient in the little things. We don't have to be ashamed to be in the learning process. The willingness to obey, in spite of fear, is, however, an essential condition. Do not be discouraged if your fear returns. We all experience ups and downs in our lives. Sometimes we have the feeling that we have really mastered something. We have learned our lesson, we have been able to overcome—and then there is a relapse. To our horror we discover that the old feeling of fear is back! But that's no reason to be discouraged. In John 16:33, shortly before the Lord Jesus starts his difficult journey of suffering and dying, he calls out to the disciples: 'In this world you will have trouble. But take heart! I have overcome the world.' What a wonderful exclamation of trust, of vision with regard to the future and of victory! This is the Son of God, who knows everything has been given to him and that the victory will be his.

Don't be discouraged when things don't seem to go well. Remind yourself of God's promises and start again.

If you don't give up, but continue to practise these principles, you will notice that a change has taken place and you are growing in maturity.

8

I Feel Guilty!

A couple of years ago I took part in a conference for Christian women where there was a discussion group on the subject, 'feelings of guilt'. The seminar was well-attended but the members of the group seemed reluctant to talk. The group leader then asked us, 'Do you ever experience vague feelings of guilt? You can't put your finger on anything that you have done wrong, but yet you feel guilty. You start losing your joy, cannot pray or read your Bible and God seems so far away. Your life is overshadowed by those terrible feelings of guilt and you honestly do not know what you have done wrong.'

To my great surprise, the discussion really exploded after this question. The majority of the women wrestled with feelings of guilt, in spite of the fact that they were all committed Christians.

The gospel brings a wonderful solution to this age-old problem of guilt. God has done everything to free us from our guilt. How is it then possible that people who have known the gospel for years, who take it seriously and proclaim the Good News to others, are still bothered by vague feelings of guilt with which they don't know what to do? Is there anything else playing a role here?

What are guilt feelings?

A feeling of guilt is an emotional indication that something is wrong, just as pain in our body warns us that something is wrong physically. Even though nobody likes pain, it still has a very valuable function in our bodies which God gave to us in order to protect us. People who have worked with leprosy patients can tell us the most horrendous stories about what happens when patients lose this feeling of pain. The fingers and toes can be nibbled away without the patient knowing it. A leg can be touching a hot oven or be scalded by hot water without the patient feeling any pain. A person who has no feeling in the lower part of his body as the result of an accident, can have an infected appendix which can burst and result in peritonitis without the person being aware of the pain that warns him of what is about to happen. No, pain is not nice and nobody is happy when her finger is caught in the car door, but still, this pain that God has given us can be a great blessing.

Well, guilt feelings are, in the same way, an alarm signal for our spirits to indicate that something is wrong, that there is something that needs our attention and perhaps a 'spiritual operation'.

However, there is a great difference between pain and guilt feelings. Pain is in most cases a trustworthy indication of something, even if it takes days of check-ups to find the cause of the pain. Pain is a function given to our bodies by God over which we have very little influence. Our conscience, however, from which our guilt feelings originate, is given by God, but is also influenced and formed by our upbringing and surroundings. Dr James Dobson compares our conscience with a group of stern little men who observe very carefully all our thoughts and deeds within us. If they spot a difference between what we do and what we should have done, they immediately protest and we receive the message: 'You should be ashamed of yourself!'

A conscience is certainly something very useful in our daily lives. It often convinces us to do that which is right, even in the little things in life. Our conscience forces us not to put things in our pocket in the supermarket and then to pass the cashier as if nothing is wrong, but instead to pay for everything. It also helps a student to start studying for his exams during a beautiful spring morning, even though he doesn't feel like studying.

Our conscience is very useful and given to us by God, but our conscience is not infallible. Our education, culture and surroundings have a great influence on our conscience. Some people do walk out of the supermarket with unpaid items in their pockets and do not feel guilty at all. Twenty years ago, most young people felt burdened by guilt feelings when they had premarital sex, while there are thousands of young people today who would find this quite normal.

When I visit my sister, who does medical work in a traditional Arab country, all the local women are fully dressed in black and heavily veiled. Exposing even the smallest part of their faces in the presence of strange men would be totally unacceptable to them. The strict little men of their conscience would give them guilt feelings the size of Mount Everest if they as much as lifted their veils. A Western woman has been brought up with a different set of values and with these high temperatures would parade in shorts, mini-skirts, sleeveless dresses or even a bikini, without feeling one ounce of guilt.

So our conscience is necessary, useful and given to us by God, but subject to education and surroundings, and, in that sense, fallible! That's why we have to learn to attune our conscience to God and his Word. This is the only way to lead a balanced Christian life and not to feel burdened by false feelings of guilt.

How can we identify false guilt feelings?

When our conscience accuses us and we feel burdened
by guilt feelings about a certain issue, we always have to
ask ourselves two questions:

1. What does the Bible say? God is very explicit in his
Word about murder, adultery, stealing, lying, and so on.
If we feel guilty about a lie, or an adulterous relation, we
do not have to look very far in order to know if this
feeling of guilt is justified or not. Our conscience accuses
us so that we will examine ourselves, confess our sin and
rid ourselves of this guilty feeling before it gets worse.

Some things we cannot trace back to the Bible, however. For instance, it may happen that a family that
brings a handicapped child into the world, struggles with
severe feelings of guilt. Parents sometimes even feel
guilty because their child is a bit 'slower' at school. They
feel that something must be definitely wrong with them,
making them fail in parenthood. Very little is written in
the Bible about this, except that the disciples also asked
Jesus if the man who was born blind had this handicap
because his parents had sinned. Jesus answered very
clearly that neither the blind man nor the parents were
guilty.

Other people are burdened by guilt when they watch
television and see the starvation in Ethiopia or the situation of refugees in other parts of the world. Now, I have
to admit that it is a good thing to be sensitive to the
needs of this world and to give abundantly from that
which we have. But it is just not on or reasonable to feel
personally responsible or guilty about all the suffering in
this world.

2. Was it my intention to do wrong? A short time ago, I
watched a television programme about mistakes made in
hospitals by doctors which had resulted in the death of

children. All the parents interviewed on this programme were burdened by great feelings of guilt with regard to the death of their child. They had thoughts like:

'I wish I had never allowed them to operate.'

'I wish I had chosen a different hospital.'

'I wish I had asked more questions about the risks involved.'

But are these feelings of guilt justified in these cases? NO! All these parents had honestly done what they thought would be the best for their child.

Satan, the accuser

Satan likes to use these feelings of guilt to torment and wound us. If you are feeling terribly guilty about something which is not your fault (like the starvation in this world), then there is no confession and forgiveness for that guilt. These false feelings of guilt might sometimes appear to be very pious, but they are in fact used by the 'father of all lies', who pretends to be 'an angel of light' and accuses us day and night in our conscience about issues for which we cannot find forgiveness, in order to devour us and to put our lives on a side-track.

Women in full-time service and false feelings of guilt

When we remember the way in which Satan can torment people and discourage them by means of false feelings of guilt, then it is obvious that women who carry responsibility in spiritual work, and the wives of pastors, missionaries and leaders, are in particular danger of being spiritually disabled by these feelings.

In general they are people with a desire to serve God. They have a tremendous feeling of responsibility and want to serve others at all times. They certainly don't want to be selfish, and under the pressure of the job and the overwhelming demands sometimes placed on them, it does sometimes happen that at a certain time they are physically and emotionally unable to cope. I have often spoken to female missionaries and wives of spiritual leaders who were absolutely drained, but it seemed that it was just not possible for them to get away for a while. They felt that their conscience would not allow them to take a break.

Last summer, I was invited, together with a number of other leaders' wives, to talk with a woman psychiatrist who specialised in the problems of missionary workers. All of us were around forty years old, most of us had been in full-time service for over twenty years and almost all of us had big families with a number of growing teenagers. Even though we were of different nationalities and worked in completely different mission fields, our problems were the same. We were tired and most of us had the feeling that the continuous pressure of constantly receiving and caring for people, the evangelism, the care of new converts, the many conferences, prayer meetings, Bible studies and the continuous lack of money, was just too much to handle.

We were surprised to discover that this Christian psychiatrist found this to be quite normal. She told us that there was only one solution to our common problem. She said: 'People of your age and with your pace of living and responsibility, have to get out once a week—for at least half a day. Go swimming, walking or play tennis, but go away. On top of that you all need one month's holiday a year, divided in two!'

We looked at one another and started laughing! Who could afford such luxury? But even if the opportunity had been there, the reaction of most women was: 'I wouldn't dare, I would be tormented by my guilt feelings!'

I still think this psychiatrist was right. There is no

other solution to these problems. Is it unbiblical to take a rest when you have come to the end of your tether? No, surely not! Is it reasonable to take a holiday when you are over-tired? Yes, absolutely! Is it wrong or selfish to take a rest from time to time? No, because I will be able to serve the Lord, my husband, my children and my brothers and sisters better.

I would almost dare to say that the more a person is committed to the Lord, and the bigger his feelings of responsibility for the business of the Lord are, the bigger the danger that false feelings of guilt will torment his life. These false feelings of guilt can sometimes result in a valuable person in God's service being neutralised through a nervous breakdown or serious physical complaints and the devil will have reached his goal in this way.

What do we do with false feelings of guilt?

Recognising and accepting that certain feelings of guilt are not biblical and reasonable is a big step in the right direction. Jeremiah 17:9,10 reminds us:

'The heart is deceitful above all things and beyond cure. Who can understand it? I the Lord search the heart and examine the mind.'

Usually we use this verse to indicate how rotten we are, and in many cases this is true. But the heart is also deceitful and beyond our understanding in its judgement of ourselves. How wonderful that God searches us and knows when our intentions were right! He knows we only wanted to do good and still felt accused.

1 John 3:20 also reminds us: '...Whenever our hearts condemn us...God is greater than our hearts, and he knows everything.'

This is wonderful. Even if our heart condemns us, God is greater. He knows and searches more than we do. He is the loving Father. He doesn't stand there with a rod behind his back waiting to punish us (like our conscience often does) for something that is neither sinful nor unreasonable! He is the good Shepherd and if we are burdened with false feelings of guilt, we will have to learn to rest with him.

Our feelings of guilt are also often inspired by fear of what other people will think of us. Even if we know and sincerely believe that the thing we said or did was correct, there can still be this vague feeling of guilt which originates out of fear of the judgement of others. It is important that we learn to recognise this and to deal with it. We are responsible to God, who is greater than our hearts and who knows everything.

Are you burdened under vague feelings of guilt? Do you feel guilty about things which you could not help and for which you cannot ask forgiveness? Does your feeling of guilt originate out of fear of others? Kick the devil out! He is the accuser ready to trap you. His aim is to make you ineffective. Put your trust in God. Let him place your feet on the Rock who is Christ. Therein lies forgiveness and freedom.

Justified feelings of guilt

God has given us our conscience as an alarm bell in case of danger. Sometimes it's a false alarm, but often the alarm signals real danger.

When I have blasted my children, when I have lost my patience, when I have been dishonest, when I have wasted my time or have been tempted into buying something I did not really need, then it is good that my conscience accuses me. But the question comes up again: 'What do I do with that guilt?' There are several possibilities:

1. I can pretend nothing is wrong, find excuses for myself and harden my heart. If I just do this often enough, the voice of my conscience will lose its power and I will deteriorate into a state of no return.

2. I can punish myself. By nature most of us will tend to do just that. If I really feel I have gone too far with something, then I will try to be extra good over the coming hours and days in order to 'make up' and win back God's 'favour'. Even though this is unbiblical, it's certainly human. But this is no solution for our guilt feelings.

3. The only correct solution for our guilt feelings that are justified lies in the essence of the gospel. The Lord Jesus did not only come down to earth to forgive us those sins we had committed before our conversion. He died for all our sins. The whole Bible is full of this truth:

'But with you there is forgiveness' (Psalm 130:4).

'Who forgives all my sins' (Psalm 103:3).

'The Lord is compassionate and gracious...He does not treat us as our sins deserve...As far as the east is from the west, so far has he removed our transgressions from us' (Psalm 103:8–12).

What do we have to do in order to obtain this forgiveness? 'If we confess our sins, he is faithful and just and will forgive us our sins and purify us from all unrighteousness' (1 John 1:9); 'And the blood of Jesus, his Son, purifies us from every sin' (1 John 1:7).

Confessing and repentance is the only solution. In the story of David and Bathsheba it is quite striking that David first of all hardens his heart and tries to cover everything up and lives with this burden of sin for a couple of months (even though he himself said that as long as he was silent his bones withered away within him). However, when the prophet Nathan tells him: 'You are the man!', then there is an immediate repentance. 'Then David said to Nathan, "I have sinned

against the Lord." Nathan replied, "The Lord has taken
away your sin" ' (2 Samuel 12:13).

David's sin was not a little thing: adultery, combined
with murder. On top of that he had tried to deceive
others, carrying on as if nothing was wrong. But when he
came to repentance, God's response was: 'Your Lord
has taken away your sin.' That is wonderful, almost too
good and too simple to be true. But this is exactly the
message of the Bible.

God's solution

Many people and many Christians suffer under the
weight of guilt feelings. I sometimes think that women
suffer even more than men. Maybe this is why so many
women do not achieve the power they would like to
possess, because these feelings of guilt constantly push
them down and make them feel miserable. Many would
say that our society actually helps women to feel guilty
by raising false expectations.

A Christian, however, should never have to live constantly with feelings of guilt. If the guilt feelings are
correct and justified, then God offers us a tremendous
and immediate solution. Lay them before him. He has
thrown our sins in the depth of the sea, and as Corrie ten
Boom said; 'He will then put up a sign: "No fishing".'

This is great! This is the core of the gospel. We don't
have to pretend that everything is okay. We don't have
to swallow tranquillisers just because we see no way out
of our guilt. We are able to confess it. We are sinners.
We do wrong, regularly. We are fallible. But that is not
the end of the story. Jesus Christ came to this world to
take the guilt upon him and to carry the death penalty
for us. That is wonderful! God can now forgive us and
accept us as beloved children while his justified claim for
punishment has been satisfied.

9

I'm Not Good Enough!

Feelings of inferiority flourish in our Western society. When I visited the Arab World and observed the way of life of the farmers and tribal people of this fascinating part in the world, I wondered how these people felt about themselves. When I put the question to my sister and brother-in-law, who have worked in that area for many years, they were not quite sure how they should answer me. Even though they have many friends in the area and have built up a feeling of trust with the local people, they could not recall having come across feelings of inferiority amongst these people; feelings which are well known to us in the West.

Is it because life is so much slower and less demanding? Is it because families and tribes are still quite close and thus individuals enjoy much more family protection? Is it the fact that school education, outward appearance or beautiful clothes are of little importance in that traditional society? Are inferiority feelings a luxury which those in the Third World cannot afford because the battle to live requires all their attention? Is it possible that their belief and trust in Allah, who arranges everything in life, has shielded them? You're free to draw your own conclusions, but I suspect that all these factors play a part.

The breakdown of this same combination in Western culture could have led to the influence of destructive feelings. Even though men also wrestle with feelings of inferiority, it appears to have reached epidemic proportions amongst women. Dr James Dobson, a specialist in the area of family problems, researched the most important reasons for depression among women. More than fifty per cent of all women surveyed admitted that feelings of inferiority were the first cause of their depression. Eighty per cent mentioned inferiority complexes among the first five causes of their depression. These were often beautiful, well educated women who certainly did not portray this image to the outside world. The survey included women from different social classes and backgrounds; mothers, housewives and working women. From my own experience in working with girls and women from many countries it is clear that this problem is not confined to non-Christians.

Most women only see two possibilities in dealing with these feelings:

1. *The reaction chosen by most Christian women is to 'withdraw'*. If you just remain in the background, never get to know new people, never give your opinion and never take the initiative, the risk of making a fool of yourself is so much lower! The safe walls of your house and your family give you protection against criticism and rejection. Not that you're now winning the battle against your feelings. You reproach and remind yourself continually that you cannot and dare not do anything. To be 'just a housewife' is not a much-praised profession in this world. If your feelings of inferiority are the main reason why you have withdrawn into your home, you will not be fulfilled by your work, but feel even more devalued, until even your husband and children can become a threat to you.

2. Another reaction is one of hatred and opposition to everything that even suggests 'male'. This reaction will not be so obvious among Christian women because this attitude would not be accepted by Christian society and would cause quite a lot of criticism. In society around us, however, we see this quite a bit. Hate and resentment are rampant in the extreme wing of feminism, and everything that is male has to suffer for the injustice done to women, which is said to have caused their inferiority complexes.

You may find this reaction with some Christian women, but they'll be much more subtle. They won't preach extreme feminism, but they will take every opportunity to criticise, undermine and hurt their husbands. Their husbands must suffer for the pain caused by inferiority feelings, for which the wives hold them responsible, consciously or subconsciously.

The causes of inferiority feelings

1. Our sinful nature and background are the deepest and most fundamental cause of people's inferiority feelings. They are deep within our fallen, sinful and 'God-separated' nature. Even small children are afraid to look foolish and are continually looking, just like their parents, for confirmation and approval of their actions. When the children grow up and go to the nursery, primary and secondary school, life becomes one big 'try not to be different' game. Their own insecurity and lack of self-worth force them to conform in order to acquire the approval of the group. If that goes well and the children are praised at home, meet the approval of their teachers and become popular among their friends, then their self-confidence will slowly but surely become stronger.

When the opposite takes place and the children only get criticised at home and laughed at, nothing seems to work in school, nobody wants to play with them, then every day is a painful confirmation of the ever-present feeling that they are 'hopeless failures'. The teenage years, which are a time of insecurity and a seeking of one's personality, become a terrible time, even for the most confident child. Rebellion, and attempts to prove themselves in all possible and impossible ways, are the only ways in which they can assert themselves. To be going against the grain, acting tough, drinking alcohol, smoking cigarettes, experimenting with sex and even drugs seem to some to be the only way to prove that you are 'somebody'! Unfortunately, this is a dead end, only leading the insecure youngster into bigger problems.

A close, loving and encouraging family is surely one of the most important factors to help the child to develop a healthy feeling of self-worth. Parents need an extra dose of wisdom and sensitivity to know when to encourage and when to admonish. Fashion, music, television and parties are issues to be looked into by any wise Christian parent. Make sure when it is at all possible, to allow the child to be a part of the group. Opinions on this will of course differ from family to family, but we should never underestimate how difficult it is for a child to have to stand alone. The exclusion from a group can leave life-long scars on a child's soul and can lead to big problems during the teenage years. It is of vital importance to spend a lot of time with your child and to ask him about his feelings.

When my children were growing up, we were very short of money and often had to rely on gifts of clothes, but I tried to avoid at all costs to force my children to wear clothes in which they felt ridiculous and old-fashioned. It is better to have only two pairs of trousers and two sweaters that are 'in' than a whole cupboard of clothes he finds revolting. If we are sensitive to these issues, get close to our children, sympathise with them, share their hurts, their joys and their loneliness they will be able to cope with life. If we talk about their feelings and help and encourage them, it will be easier for them to find and understand where the border is of what we as Christians can do and where we have to take a stand.

I am convinced that if we tackle the inborn feelings of insecurity of our children in this way, then we will experience God's grace and help and see them grow up into stable, young Christians.

2. Judging people by appearances. A beautiful face and a good figure all belong to the essential features upon which people are judged and judge themselves. The odd thing is that even beautiful is never beautiful enough. One person thinks her nose is too long, another thinks her teeth are too big. Most girls and women think they are too fat, but if they are slim they think they are too skinny. I have always been the skinny kind and I remember very clearly the remarks that were made about me in school: 'Skin and bone', 'she looks the same front and back', and so on. I always wished I had a few more curves, but now I discover that others, who I think have an ideal figure, think themselves too fat. There is no objective measure and outward appearance is for many women a never-ending source of inferiority feelings.

3. Judging people by intelligence and education. I think that with most girls beauty is more important than intelligence while with boys it is perhaps the other way round. Our school systems demand a lot from our children. The daily frustration of a child who doesn't make it in the system can, in the end, lead to very negative effects. To receive low grades every day during your schooling strengthens the awful feelings within you that you are simply stupid. Even if your parents tell you differently and say that each person has different gifts, those bad grades still confirm to you that they are wrong and you were right in your judgement of yourself.

Many grown-ups are now saddled with inferiority feelings they developed while still at school. They know that a lack of schooling will influence their child for the rest of his life. It is common knowledge that fathers often pressure their children into doing the impossible because they want their child to succeed where they failed. Many women consider themselves to be stupid. Their isolation in the home with small children, and thoughtless comments from their husbands about their lack of knowledge or insight into certain issues, constantly develops those feelings of inferiority to the point of no return.

4. Coping with failure. Constant failure can lead to immense feelings of inferiority. Our society is geared for sex and beauty, intelligence and success! If you can't cope with certain areas in life, the seeds for an inferiority complex are quickly sown.

The key issue in a man's life is his job. If he fails at his job, he considers himself a failure in life. Thus, long periods of unemployment cause enormous dents in people's self-confidence.

For women the key issue is their family. If they fail at making their marriage work—even if they've tried their very best—they feel a deep sense of failure. The knowledge of not having been able to save your marriage, the fact that you were unable to keep your husband, that he whom you loved and in whom you had invested your life doesn't want you any more, or exchanged you for somebody else, often leads to a woman losing the last of her self-respect.

5. Clinical depression. Sometimes feelings of inferiority go beyond the sort I am talking about here, and result in clinical depression. No one knows why one woman is able to recover from an inferiority complex, while another needs medical, expert help. Hormonal factors or childhood history may all play a part. What is important is that if your inferiority feelings are totally extreme and irrational, and especially if you feel tempted towards suicide or violence, you should not be afraid to seek medical help immediately.

GETTING RID OF INFERIORITY FEELINGS

It is clear that many of us live with feelings of insecurity and inferiority. Some people are bothered by it more than others, some people know how to compensate for it better than others. For some everything in life seems to be going against them. All of this influences how we feel and what we think about ourselves.

Even though this is all very normal and human, as a Christian you can't help asking yourself whether this should change after you've accepted Christ. Paul says that we became a new creation in Christ, the old has passed away, and the new has come. At some point we realise that feelings of inferiority don't fit in with being a new creation.

God, not happiness, is the ultimate goal

'But seek first his kingdom and his righteousness, and all these things will be given to you as well' (Matthew 6:33), are the words of the Lord Jesus about the way people worry about themselves.

' "Love the Lord your God with all your heart and with all your soul and with all your mind and with all your strength." The second [most important command] is this: "Love your neighbour as yourself." There is no commandment greater than these' (Mark 12:30–31).

According to Jesus, everything in our lives should be geared towards loving God and, next, to loving our neighbour. This leaves little space for endless worrying about ourselves.

Paul admonishes us again and again, as does Peter, that we have to do everything for God's glory, and in the name of the Lord Jesus, thanking God the Father, so that God will be glorified through Jesus Christ.

The honour and glorifying of God should be the focal point of our thinking, not our own status. We usually think that by giving more time to ourselves and by doing everything possible to be respected in life, we will be better off. In Mark 8:35 the Lord Jesus says, however: 'For whoever wants to save his life will lose it, but whoever loses his life for me and for the gospel will save it.'

This is a different language! This is so contrary to the way we think. Through all our complexes and feelings of inferiority we are continually busy with ourselves, boosting our egos, re-establishing ourselves and trying to regain our honour. And now the Lord Jesus says just the opposite! Let go, surrender yourself to me, be the least, become the smallest, lose your life for my name's sake, because this is the only way to keep it!

God attaches great value to us

I find it quite interesting comparing God's opinion of us to the way we look at ourselves.

1. Humankind, the crown to God's creation. God created us after his own image (Genesis 1:26) and God was pleased. After the creation of nature, humankind was God's pride and glory, the most beautiful and most precious thing he had ever made.

Even after the 'fall' God still holds humankind in high

esteem. Humankind is still the most beautiful and precious creation. In Genesis 9:6 God says that though people are making a mess of life, they are still precious in God's sight, for they are made in the image of God. Therefore their lives have high value. In Psalm 8 David looks at the sky and marvels at the greatness of the universe. People look so small and insignificant compared with all that. But David also knows God as a personal friend who attaches much value to human life. For that reason he exclaims, inspired by the Holy Spirit: 'You made man a little lower than the heavenly beings and crowned him with glory and honour. You made him ruler over the works of your hands; you put everything under his feet.' This attitude leaves little space for inferiority feelings!

2. Fallen people are the subject of God's overwhelming love! God loved people so much that he, even after people became disobedient and were separated from God by their sins, did everything to save them, even to the point where he gave his only Son. Through the precious blood of Jesus, God, who had created us, bought us back.

3. People who accept God's salvation will be loved by God and overloaded with gifts. The New Testament is full of verses showing us what God has done for us. God has saved us from death and given us life eternal. He no longer condemns us, but makes us into a new creation. He has blessed us with all spiritual blessings and makes us more than conquerors. He gives us strength to be able to cope with anything and made us fellow citizens with God. He even gives us his own holy Spirit to dwell within us, to lead us, to help us and to give us power.

To put it bluntly, we are not a bunch of nitwits, but a chosen people, a royal priesthood, a people belonging to

God! It is quite clear that the biblical vision for a person as God's creation, even as a fallen creature and even more so as a liberated and loved child of God, does not match our own feelings of inferiority.

What is the difference between humility and inferiority?

This is a question that many Christians battle with and which creates confusion and misunderstanding. It sounds so spiritual to say all the time that you are worth nothing, that you are only a miserable sinner who cannot do anything good! Many Christians have the habit of saying: 'I didn't accomplish that, it was the Lord.' Even though we understand that they want to say that God gave them the power and the grace to achieve something, it is still not expressed in the proper way. To an outsider this remark sounds ridiculous. If someone has done a great job, that's it, he's done a great job!

The example of Jesus always impresses me. Jesus was the perfect image of humility and dependence upon the Father. He continually emphasises his unity with his Father. He talks about the fact that he does not seek his own glory. But there is no trace of any inferiority feelings with Jesus. He knows who he is, the Son of God, the Saviour of the world! In that he stands firm and immovable, even though the people attack him from all sides and nobody sees anything in him any more. When Jesus voluntarily takes the place of a servant and washes the disciples' feet before they take their seats at the table, he does not do this because he feels inferior and sees himself only as a 'foot-washer'. No, the opposite is true. He says to his disciples: 'You call me "Teacher" and "Lord", and rightly so, for that is what I am' (John 13:13).

He knows who he is, Master and Lord, and he still washes those feet because he is humble of heart. In the same way we can know who we are, and still remain humble. It is not unspiritual to know and acknowledge your position as a beloved child of God and to be thankful for the gifts and qualities God has given you and to be happy with them. This is not pride. A thankful self-acceptance can go hand in hand with a humble heart and an attitude of servanthood, just like Jesus.

We see this same attitude in Paul. In Christ he has a healthy feeling of self-worth. He calls himself an apostle called by God and even says that he is not in the least inferior to these super-apostles (2 Corinthians 12:11)! This might sound a little bit arrogant to us. But it wasn't meant that way and God even allowed this rather daring remark to have its place in the Bible! Paul, at the same time, knows that he is fully dependent upon God and has counted everything that was to his advantage as nothing for Christ's sake! Somewhere else he calls himself the least of the apostles.

When Paul speaks in Romans 7 about the fact that in his flesh there is no good thing and that he is a miserable person, he does not say this because he is suddenly overwhelmed by a terrible feeling of inferiority. Romans 8 is the proof of this, as it is a song of victory and assurance in God's power and love. No, in Romans 7 he is speaking about his sinful nature, about the sin living within him. He even says: 'As it is, it is no longer I myself who do it, but it is sin living in me' (Romans 7:17).

At other times Paul speaks about the difference between our old nature and the new one. He sees the old nature as our personality before we got to know the Lord Jesus; giving in to sin, and controlled by sin! After our conversion however, the old has passed away and the new has come! That new personality, cleansed and made holy by God, growing towards God and resembling Jesus more and more each day through the indwelling of the

Holy Spirit, is pleasing to God. God likes to give that new person a ministry and let her become a co-worker (2 Corinthians 5:17—6:1). There is no reason to feel inferior, but there is reason for thankfulness and a motivation to serve God in this life, with heads held high and brimming with confidence!

To deny yourself and to take up the cross to follow Jesus is not synonymous with despising, hating or humiliating yourself. Jesus denied himself and literally took his cross upon him. However, he knew that he had overcome the world and that he was Lord and Master. The Lord Jesus did not take the suffering and the humiliation upon him because he did not like himself, or because it gave him pleasure to inflict pain upon himself. No, the reason was far beyond that. The aim was to suffer and die to bear the punishment for people and to bring salvation to them. If the Bible requires us to have that same attitude as the Lord Jesus and to deny ourselves and take up our cross, the aim is the same. God does not require us to deny ourselves because we are a hopeless bunch. No, he asks us to deny ourselves to further the King's business. He wants us to put aside our own interests in order to, just like Jesus, serve others that they might know Christ.

A short time ago there was a programme on television about 'miracle children', who had various special talents. One of them was a twelve-year-old tennis champion. One girl played the violin and had played at famous violin concerts since she was ten years old. What struck me more than anything else were the great sacrifices these children had had to make to be where they now were. Training for four to five hours a day was the minimum. Of course they also had to study their other subjects, even though they did not have a normal school education. Playing, friends, relaxation and holidays were luxuries unknown to them. Even though they were very young, they displayed, for the sake of their extraordinary talent and the hope of a famous future, a great amount of self-discipline and willingness to give up. This is what the Bible means by the term 'self-denial'! The children did not sacrifice their friends and play because they had an inferiority complex and thought that nobody would want to play with them! No, they were totally convinced about their talent and their future.

God wants us Christians to meet life in that same way. Paul says in 1 Corinthians 9:19–27 that he denies himself all kinds of things voluntarily and disciplines himself to save some people and to reach the goal that God has set for him.

I am fully convinced that inferiority feelings are not biblical. Discover for yourself in the New Testament what wonderful privileges God has given every Christian and that God wants to use us in this world in order to execute his plan.

When I became a Christian during my teenage years, I suffered like most teenagers from the usual feelings of insecurity and inferiority. When God's Spirit came to dwell within me and I began to understand via the Bible how highly God valued me, these feelings melted away! They made place for a thankful acceptance of God's value of me. But some people may need to take more positive action.

What can I do to conquer my feelings of inferiority?

1. Decide to let them go. We often cherish these feelings. We are continually busy worrying about ourselves. This is not correct and not biblical. Every time you discover that you are worrying about yourself, stop it and direct your thoughts elsewhere. Take the decision each time to be prepared to give up your life for Christ's sake. You will slowly discover that in this way you are gaining a new life!

2. Train yourself to concentrate upon God. God's greatest command is that we love him and that everything we do should be to his glory. If you start worrying about yourself again, if you are tormenting yourself by remembering the times you made yourself ridiculous, instead direct your thoughts towards God. Memorise scriptures, stick them above the kitchen sink! Start every day with God, choose a really inspiring verse about God's power, God's love, God's greatness or God's grace. Reach out to this verse during the course of the day in order that it might mark your day.

We may have a wonderful image of God. We may say with our mouths that God is almighty, omnipresent and all-knowing, but if this knowledge does not go down from our head to our heart and our emotions, it will not be of any help to us in our daily life. Train yourself, exercise yourself to concentrate upon God and upon all he is.

3. Concentrate upon your neighbour with a giving love. This is the second command and fulfills, together with the first command, all the laws and commands that God has given to people. It is healthy and useful for us to give our attention and time to other people. If you have the tendency to think yourself pathetic and inferior, look for someone who has less than you and who needs your help and love. You will then start to see your own life in a different perspective and will have less time to think about yourself.

Also, the fact that you feel useful and mean something to somebody will help you in this area. When I had to remain in hospital for two weeks after an operation, I found myself in a terrible state. I had suffered several complications in health, I had become allergic to all kinds of medicines, and now this! The first days after the operation I was sick and miserable, but when my fever dropped somewhat and I was able to move about a little bit, I started to notice the three other patients in my ward. Pretty soon it became obvious that each had a story of sadness, failure, sickness and insecurity. My heart opened up for these poor women and I realised how difficult life can be for some people.

My days in the hospital took on a completely different perspective. I was reminded how privileged I was being a Christian, to have a conscience that is free from guilt, and a life that is reasonably uncomplicated because it is lived according to God's commandments. Assurance of my salvation and the love of fellow Christians took on a new meaning. God gave me love for these women and a ministry of comfort and encouragement. When I eventually left the hospital, I took many precious memories home with me.

4. Continue to evaluate yourself honestly and concentrate on developing your gifts. We are all different, but this should never be a reason to feel inferior. God loves this diversity. In the creation he exhibited all his creativity by making each cell, each snowflake, each flower, each person and each animal different. Also in the new creation and in his new plan—the Church—he showed an enormous amount of diversity. We all received different gifts. In 1 Corinthians 12, Paul compares it with the different parts of our body, each part having its own function.

If you have discovered your gifts, started to exercise them, and realise that God wants to use you, then you will begin to understand that it is not necessary to compare yourself with others. God loves you, just as you are. He has given you gifts which he wants to use. He made a specific place in his Body and a perfect plan for your life. If you learn to accept that and to grow in his way, your feelings of inferiority will disappear.

10

I'm Being Criticised!

'He that builds upon the street, many masters has to meet', goes an old proverb. This is certainly true for everyone who starts walking on the road with Christ. If all kinds of new things are happening in your life, if you slowly but surely see victory take place and want to make these things known to those around you, you can be sure there will be 'spectators'.

Unfortunately, not all spectators are positive in their comments. If criticism only came from the corner of sceptical atheists, we would be able to swallow it. We could never expect them to understand our actions and motivations! The Lord Jesus himself prepared us for that when he said: 'In this world you will have trouble. But take heart! I have overcome the world' (John 16:33). He also said that a slave is not above his master, and that we shouldn't expect better treatment than he received. That is clear. The disciples considered it an honour to suffer for Jesus. If the Lord gives us strength and grace, we would perhaps also be prepared for that.

But it is more difficult when it is not the atheists, but our fellow Christians, brothers and sisters in the Lord Jesus, who start criticising our well-intended and honest attempts to serve God's kingdom. Yet it is something that happens regularly. It can make you so sad, it can discourage you so much that you're tempted to throw in the towel. That's why I want to warn you and hand you the right spiritual weapons for this part of our battle. I have been amazed to see how much emphasis the Bible places on criticism.

Criticism, the sickness of our time

Even though it is clear that there has been criticism from the moment that there were sinful people, I still think that in our time, and in our part of the world, it has grown beyond all proportions. If sinful, limited people decide to do certain things, it is logical that other sinful, limited people won't agree with them. It is normal and even necessary to be able to express criticism in the right way. If we look at the world's totalitarian states, we realise that democracy, with its inbuilt possibility for criticism, can protect us from lots of misery. This is even true with regard to Christian churches and missions. If criticism is forbidden or excluded, there is a great danger that a church or a group under the leadership of a strong leader can change into a dangerous sect. The television pictures of the many people who died in Jonestown in British Guyana, in a mass suicide of a whole religious cult on the orders of their leader, will be present in the minds of people for a long time as an example of how things can deteriorate when no questions can be asked.

But if a society, church or group is infiltrated by an attitude of criticising everything in a destructive way, then something is fundamentally wrong. This destroying spirit of criticism has unfortunately not limited itself to worldly issues. It's a part of our education and infiltrates our way of thinking, life-style, and so on. It is logical that if we then become Christians, we will bring this way of thinking into our Christian lives. Paul admonishes us to be transformed by the renewal of our mind, but that takes time!

Often the criticism concentrates on issues that are not absolutely vital to life. If you search your own heart and see in which areas you are criticising others, you will probably agree that it usually concerns everyday things. We often measure others by our own standards. Very often our criticism is directed to material things. 'John and Mary bought new furniture! I wonder how they could afford it. They should have saved the money for their kids' education, or given it to the church!'

Cars are an endless source of jealousy and criticism. If somebody drives a very old car we think he is handling things irresponsibly. If he buys a new car we think this is extravagant. Clothes are also an unlimited source of criticism! Skirts are too short or too long! Necklines are too low or styles old-fashioned! High heels are only to attract attention but square heels belong to the last century! Sweaters are too loose or too tight and sexy!

We can spend hours criticising our neighbours or sisters from the church. The education of children, drinking or not drinking a glass of wine, spending of household money, being too 'churchy' or too 'free', being 'evangelical' or 'charismatic'; these are all things about which we can gossip. If somebody has the audacity to wander from the well-worn paths of society and start doing something 'different' in a new dependence upon the Lord, he or she has to be prepared for a flood of questions and criticism.

God describes in Jeremiah 9 the marks of a society that does not want to listen to him any more. He is not talking about the Philistines or one of the other heathen countries but about his own chosen people. The description is shocking!

' "They do not acknowledge me," declares the Lord. "Beware of your friends; do not trust your brothers. For every brother is a deceiver and every friend a slanderer. Friend deceives friend, and no-one speaks the truth. They have taught their tongues to lie; they weary themselves with sinning. You live in the midst of deception; in their deceit they refuse to acknowledge me," declares the Lord...Their tongue is a deadly arrow' (Jeremiah 9:3–8).

This is what can become of people who have known God, his love and his forgiveness, but who lose control of their tongues. This is difficult to understand, but it's unfortunately reality. That this is not God's idea and God's plan is clear. Satan is called the 'accuser of our brothers' in Revelation 12:10, 'who accuses them before our God day and night.' He takes great delight in playing people against one another and making them accuse one another. He's extremely pleased when they are Christians and still allow themselves to be manipulated by him. It saves him quite a bit of work if we accuse one another. He knows therefore how to remind us of every minute detail where our brothers and sisters stray from the 'norm', in order to encourage us to accuse them.

The interesting thing is that God gives us a lot of individual freedom. God sees the heart. If the heart is sincere, full of love and dedication to him, then God allows us freedom in many aspects! Study your Bible and find out more about this freedom which God offers to us. God doesn't accuse David about his luxury palace, his horses and wagons, his silver and his gold, not even about his wives. God even says to David in 2 Samuel 12:8: 'And if all of this had been too little, I would have given you even more.' But when David takes his neighbour's wife, gets rid of the neighbour, and covers the whole thing up, then God takes action.

Satan, however, looks for the details and often uses just the things in which God gave us individual freedom for his own destructive purposes. I don't think that God is really interested in whether we drive a Honda or a

Mercedes, or whether we wear blue jeans or a skirt. If God is not interested in all that, why do we Christians use these things to criticise one another? I even get the impression, from studying the Bible, that God loves all this variety in life. Satan, on the other hand, likes nothing better than seeing us criticise anyone who doesn't think and act the same way we do.

If we are honest, we have to admit that our judgements of others often originate from our own insecurity and feelings of inferiority. Bitterness, narrow-mindedness, misunderstandings and dishonest comparisons are sometimes also the source of criticism. However, none of these things are inspired by God. Our negative, critical attitude hurts God more than the details that cause the criticism. That's also what Jesus means when he speaks about the plank of wood and the speck of sawdust in our brother's eye (Matthew 7:1–5). He warns us not to judge others too quickly. The speck of the detail we see in the life of the other person is much less important than the plank in our own lives; the plank of a critical attitude. Let's start to deal with that plank; that plank of criticism, negative attitude and the sharp, judging tongue. What a radical change would take place if we started spring-cleaning in our churches by removing these planks of criticism!

Justified criticism

Do we then accept everything and leave things the way they are? Don't we have any responsibility to point out each other's mistakes, sins and errors? Of course we have this responsibility, but this is not criticism. The Bible says: 'If your brother sins against you, go and show him his fault' (Matthew 18:15).

That's so difficult! We would much rather tell others about it than approach the person in question and tell him what's wrong. But no matter how difficult this may seem, it is the biblical approach to dealing with sin. Concerning the thousand small irritations and differences between Christians, the command is: 'Accept one another' and 'Carry each other's burdens' (Romans 15:7, Galatians 6:2).

If we are dealing with actual sin and wrong-doing, we have to admonish one another, but as Paul says, 'Restore him gently. But watch yourself, or you also may be tempted' (Galatians 6:1). When we look at our own lives, we realise only too well that we don't really have a right to speak. Of course we will experience similar temptations as the person we have just 'caught out'. On the other hand, this should not be a reason to keep silent! We have a spiritual obligation to help the other person! But we can go to them, realising that we are weak and have the same tendency towards doing evil. The only honest and spiritual attitude in which we can say something to the other person is in deep humility. Proverbs 25:15 says: 'A gentle tongue can break a bone.'

Among our wide circle of acquaintances, I have two friends who apply this principle strictly. It is no use going to them with a juicy episode of gossip. When I told one of them recently how a mutual friend had put me on the spot several times by cancelling an appointment at the last minute without a good reason, he asked me: 'Did you point this out to her?' I swallowed, murmured a few excuses and felt a bit deflated because I knew he was right. Even though I was upset and irritated about these cancellations, I should not have told a third person. Fortunately he admonished me in a friendly manner. He said: 'Look, Toos, your telling me is not improving the situation one bit. You're not lightening your frustrations, and she won't learn anything from this. The next time this happens you tell her directly how you feel about this situation. Ask her how she can do something like that to you.' Even though I had to swallow when he told me so frankly where I had gone wrong, I realised that he was right and I respected his sincere, honest and friendly rebuke.

'Like an ear-ring of gold or an ornament of fine gold is a wise man's rebuke to a listening ear' (Proverbs 25:11, 12). This is the biblical equivalent of reproving someone and accepting that reproof: an ornament of fine gold, precious, of great value, a gem, an art! Shall we apply ourselves to this art? It won't be easy, it is going to cost us something! But it will spare us a lot of misery! What a relief it would be if you were sure that nobody was talking about you behind your back. Does this sound like Utopia? Perhaps, but it is still the biblical pattern. The well-known proverb 'improve the world and start with yourself' should be applied here. We would much rather make the other person stop criticising us, but that is not within our power. The only thing we can do is to apply this rule in our own lives. If we have had the habit of talking about others for years, then it will be very difficult to change. The only way to get rid of this nasty habit might be to ask somebody to warn you whenever you are tempted to 'fall back'.

There was an occasion during my years at Bible college when we went through a very difficult time. Many things had gone wrong. Some students were sent away and those of us who were left, started to realise how negative and critical our attitude had become. We felt the college was bad, too expensive and too strict. The food was lousy, the teachers hopeless and the lectures boring. Actually, we didn't quite understand how we had come to adopt this very negative and unspiritual attitude. Hadn't we all come to the college with high ideals and great expectations to get to know God better and to be built up in our faith?

One morning, our director called us together. He told

us how upset he was by what had happened and how worried he was about the negative atmosphere. He expressed his regret for the wrong he had done and asked us to forgive him. We were all impressed. But that was not the end of it. He told us that he realised he was being criticised and wanted to speak to each student individually. So off we went, one after the other. I don't remember anything of the conversation we had, but certainly remember feeling stupid and guilty when faced by this big, friendly and intelligent man listening to my criticism.

We had a student meeting that very afternoon, and expressed our shock at the morning's events. We realised that most of the guilt lay with us and we had to change our attitude drastically.

We were scheduled to start the summer holidays the following week, and knew that we couldn't come back in September with the same attitude. If we did it would rub off on the new students, so we had to take drastic steps. We made a commitment to adopt a more positive attitude and not entertain any negative thoughts. We would also make a point of admonishing one another in a loving and friendly manner.

What a change! When we returned in September it seemed as if we were playing a game. We were enthusiastic about everything, praised our lecturers and spoke only good of everything and everybody. It bordered on the ridiculous! But it worked! The new students looked at us in amazement, but adapted quickly to this highly positive attitude. When one of them had the audacity to criticise the lecture on biblical geography given by our director, he was so quickly confronted by the rest of us that he never tried again. Between us as older students there was a covenant. If someone said something only slightly in the direction of the old critical spirit, we only had to look at him or her to make our feelings known.

The amazing thing was that when we decided not to criticise any more and had agreed to practise a more positive attitude, it seemed as if the circumstances also changed. The lectures were no longer so boring and our teachers and the director appeared to be fantastic people who came to mean a lot to many of us.

I will never forget those last few months in Bible college. They were positive and constructive. Of all the lessons I had learned during that time, this one was the clearest: 'Ask each other's help to break the habit of criticism; it works effectively and quickly. If something is truly wrong, mention it to the person concerned in a friendly way and in humility. Learn, with the help of others, to talk positively.' When we train ourselves to talk positively we will also start thinking positively. From this positive thinking we will logically start to speak positively again and then we are where we want to be. 'For out of the overflow of the heart the mouth speaks. The good man brings good things out of the good stored up in him, and the evil man brings evil things out of the evil stored up in him. But I tell you that men will have to give account on the day of judgement for every careless word they have spoken. For by your words you will be acquitted, and by your words you will be condemned' (Matthew 12:34–37).

Unjustified criticism

What happens if we are criticised unjustly? The Bible describes in some unusual ways how a person feels who is unjustly criticised: 'Reckless words pierce like a sword' (Proverbs 12:18); 'Like a club or a sword or a sharp arrow is the man who gives false testimony against his neighbour. Like a bad tooth or a lame foot is reliance on the unfaithful in times of trouble' (Proverbs 25:18,19); 'I have become like broken pottery. For I hear the slander of many; there is terror on every side; they conspire against me and plot to take my life' (Psalm 31:12–14); and 'All my enemies whisper together against me; they imagine the worst for me… Even my close friend, whom I trusted, he who shared my bread, has lifted up his heel against me' (Psalm 41:7,9).

Have you ever discovered that a friend whom you trusted had betrayed you? Do you know the feeling when people are talking about you behind your back, they slander you and gossip about you while you sincerely loved them and only wanted to do good? Indeed, those words work like a sword, they pierce your heart! They are like clubs, like swords, like sharp arrows, all of them murder weapons to kill you. You feel like broken pottery; a broken plate, a broken glass. That sudden feeling of deep pain is like a broken tooth and a lame foot. You feel unable to go on. All you want to do is to sit down and cry. So strong is the feeling that overwhelms you when friends, brothers and sisters whom you have trusted, turn against you and criticise you unjustly!

Take comfort, you are in good company. Not only David and Solomon knew the misery of criticism. The Lord Jesus himself is described to us in Hebrews 12:3 as the one who 'endured such opposition from sinful men'. They tried all kinds of tricks on him! He did nothing but good, but whatever he did, they had something to criticise. In Matthew 11 he shows us that it is not a matter of what you do or not do, that determines the measure of criticism. The attitude of the people who want to run you down is the determining factor.

Even in this case the criticism is about the daily things like eating and drinking. First John the Baptist had come, a great prophet, an eccentric fellow. He did not eat, except some locusts. He did not drink, certainly no alcohol! And what did the people say? 'He has a demon.' Then the Son of Man came and behaved in a very normal

way! He sat down at the table with all kinds of people.
He liked fried fish, straight from the fire. He also drank a
little wine when he was visiting with friends. He even
changed water into wine when a wedding threatened to
become a great failure. And what did the people say?
'This is the kind of person we can identify with'? Oh no!
They said: 'He is a glutton and a drunkard, a friend of
tax collectors and "sinners".' Now I ask you, can you
make head or tail of that? I can't!

The Lord Jesus told this to show us that indeed there
is neither head nor tail. The question is not one of doing
something right or wrong. If people want to slander,
then they will slander, irrespective of what you do. With
the Lord Jesus it was even so bad that the more good he
did, the more angry people became. At the end even his
friend, with whom he had shared everything day and
night for three years, turned against him. This 'friend'
sold him for thirty silver coins. He betrayed him with a
kiss to the people who wanted to kill him. Terrible,
inconceivable; but it happened to the Son of God who
did not know sin and had never committed sin. No, you
are not alone. The Lord Jesus experienced it all. He was
betrayed and abandoned by all the people he loved. If
the same thing happens to us in a small way, this means
that we are allowed to follow in the footsteps of Jesus;
that we can have a small taste of his suffering.

The apostle Paul did not have an easy passage either.
He was violently criticised not only by the heathens and
Jews, but also by Christians. The people he had taken
the gospel to, for whom he had risked his life, for whom
he had given everything in order that they might find
Christ, those people later turned against him and criticised him. In 1 Corinthians Paul writes about this. At
first he says that he does not care what the people say
about him, and that it is more important what God says
about him (1 Corinthians 4:3–5). However, he adds in

verse 9 that it seems to him that God had given them the last place—foolish for Christ's sake! But, he says, 'When we are slandered, we answer kindly.' This is not easy, not even for Paul. In chapter 9 he comes back to it and asks the Corinthians why they have different standards for Barnabas and him than they have for the other apostles! He doesn't understand it, it makes him sad and he tries to convince them about the fact that he has been sincere in everything he has done.

It seems that the issue is not easily solved because in 2 Corinthians 10, 11 and 12 Paul returns to this subject again and again. He is tempted to sum up all he has done for them for the sake of the gospel and all the spiritual experiences he has had. In chapter 12 he even becomes sarcastic when he mentions that he is not in the least inferior to the 'super-apostles' and cries out: 'How were you inferior to the other churches, except that I was never a burden to you? Forgive me this wrong!' He admits honestly that if someone has difficulty with these things, he should be burning inwardly! (2 Corinthians 11:29).

Do you know that feeling, that your heart and cheeks are burning with pain because the people you loved are so unjust to you and are judging you? Paul experienced this. He found it difficult to cope with. Sometimes he was able to leave it with the Lord and remain friendly. Sometimes it came back like a stab of severe pain and he defended himself, using his sharp pen because the hurt was burning in his soul. The man who spoke to us about the fruit of the Spirit, about forgiveness and bearing with one another, has—inspired by God—described the battle with the pain of lack of appreciation and criticism.

How to cope with criticism

What does the Bible say we have to do with the criticism that comes our way?

1. Rejoice and be glad... 'When people insult you, per-
secute you and falsely say all kinds of evil against you
because of me... Great is your reward in heaven' (Matthew 5:11,12).

This is not easy, but quite clear! Our human reaction
is to give up and to withdraw in our hurt and bitterness.
Never in my life have I battled so much with discourage-
ment and depression as during the time when we were
flooded with criticism. The problem is also the fact that
we are not without sin like the Lord Jesus. In every
accusation is a bit of truth from which we can learn and
change. And in the midst of all the bitter words that are
poured out over us we do not always remain friendly. If
people are hell-bent at getting at you, you only have to
lose your cool once and your adversaries have achieved
what they set out to do. Then you'll have the devil
breathing down your neck saying you're a hopeless case
and not worth much. The Lord Jesus however invites
you not to let your head hang down. He says rejoice and
be glad, for it has positive results in your life. All the
people he calls blessed in Matthew 5 are people who are
having difficulties:

> Blessed are the poor in spirit;
> Blessed are those who mourn;
> Blessed are those who hunger and thirst for righteous-
> ness;
> Blessed are the peacemakers;
> Blessed are those who are persecuted because of right-
> eousness;
> Blessed are you when people insult you... and falsely say
> all kinds of evil against you...

Our problems, worries and our rowing against the tide
propel us closer to God. They don't leave us without
fruit for this life. That's why James says: 'Consider it
pure joy, my brothers, whenever you face trials of many

kinds, because you know that the testing of your faith develops perseverance' (James 1:2).

Have you been wrongly accused or criticised? Has your husband been abused and slandered? Are you sitting in your corner, bitter and broken? Come on! Get up! Our faith is tested and our fruit will be perseverance and our reward is in heaven.

2. Refer back to your position in Christ. 'Therefore, there is now no condemnation for those who are in Christ Jesus' (Romans 8:1). Even if the whole world condemns you, God has accepted you. That's great, now hold on to it!

You belong to:

*A chosen people and
*A royal priesthood (1 Peter 2:9)
*For he chose us in him before the creation of the world (Ephesians 1:4).

Our human ego is very vulnerable; we are easily hurt by criticism. Let's be more rooted in our position in Jesus Christ! That is our assurance. Paul calls it an 'anchor for the soul'. Throw out your anchor on the rock who is Christ. He never changes. Okay, I admit we make mistakes, we often behave badly, and we are vulnerable! But surely we knew this when we became Christians? That's why we threw out our anchor on a different spot. Let's stick to that. David comes to the same conclusion in Psalm 31: he initially pictures himself as broken pottery, with terror on every side and surrounded by conspiracy and slander. Then he cries out: 'But I trust in you, O Lord; I say, "You are my God." My times are in your hands... How great is your goodness, which you have stored up for those who fear you, which you bestow in the sight of men on those who take refuge in you. In the shelter of your presence you hide them from the intrigues of men; in your dwelling you keep them safe from the strife of tongues' (Psalm 31:14–20).

3. Remember that we are accountable to God, and God sees the heart. In his discussions with the Corinthians, Paul tells them: 'You are looking only on the surface of things' (2 Corinthians 10:7), and therein lies the cause of a lot of criticism. People judge what they see. But often they are not aware of the motives of the other person. However, if you are criticised in your absence and you do not get the chance to explain why you did it that way, then it is comforting to know that God not only judges the outside and the end results, but also knows our heart. Our deepest thoughts and motives are known to him. John even says that God is greater than our hearts and he knows everything (1 John 3:20). In the end we are accountable to God and fortunately he doesn't judge on first impressions. Everything is uncovered and laid bare before him (Hebrews 4:13). If we were more conscious of this we would not become so preoccupied with the way in which others judge us. For Jesus, this was indisputable. That's why he did not even defend himself before the people who falsely accused him. He was silent, convinced that God had everything in his hands and that he would judge righteously.

4. Take courage; God does not forget what we have done for him. If people level criticism at our ministry or reject us because they disagree with our actions, it is comforting to know that God does not forget what we have done in his name. It is human nature to easily forget twenty good, fruitful years if something happens that evokes criticism, division and disunity. It makes you wonder whether all that you have done was in vain or of no value. Take courage! Even if it seems to be that way, and even if people tend to think so, God does not!

'God is not unjust; he will not forget your work and the love you have shown him as you have helped his people and continue to help them' (Hebrews 6:10).

God is different to people. He judges each man's work impartially (1 Peter 1:17). We judge partially! If we like people, if they think the way we think and if they are our friends, then we look favourably upon their work! But if we dislike people, if they give us trouble and we do not find them sympathetic to our cause, then we find it very difficult to see the positive aspects of their work. It's a good thing that God is so different and impartial. He doesn't forget the details. He remembers even better than we do the things we have done out of love for him. Don't allow criticism to pressurise you into thinking that what you have done was in vain. That's a cheap trick from the devil himself who is out to destroy us.

5. *Give it time.* Time will not tell us everything, but it will tell us what we need to know! Paul says that a servant of God must prove faithful (1 Corinthians 4:2).

People who destructively criticise will have to, in the long run, prove if they were just or not in their criticism. If you are convinced that you have done or said the right thing, then hang in there, even if you are slandered for it. The proof will come!

Do not be tempted to take revenge. Revenge is not always murder or manslaughter. You can take revenge by picking up the phone and telling a few home truths about that woman who has criticised you. Don't do that. It will not solve the problem. The only result is a vicious cycle of spitefulness and accusations, which results in more hurt. Apply the same rule I mentioned earlier. 'Leave it alone and it will leave you alone.' Surrender it to God, he says that if there is place for revenge, he will do it in his own time (Romans 12:19). If you have acted in the right way with a clear conscience, then it will prove itself. Be quiet and give it time.

6. *Love your enemies*. Time and again we see how different our thinking is to God's thinking. Not only do we have to rejoice and be happy when people cause trouble for us, not only should we not take our rights into our own hands when we are unjustly judged, but the Lord takes it even further. He commands us to love our enemies, and to pray for those who ill-treat us (Luke 6:27,28). Paul makes this very practical in Romans 12. Do something good for those that bring trouble into your life. 'If your enemy is hungry, feed him; if he is thirsty, give him something to drink. In doing this, you will heap burning coals on his head' (Romans 12:20).

When we had some trouble with a family in our church, the Lord reminded me time and again of these verses. I tried to find good excuses not to have to go but in the end I just had to obey. After a lot of prayer and with trembling knees I set out on my 'burning-coal mission'. When I rang the bell, one of the children opened the door. I went in and stepped into a room with people who had obviously just been talking about me. A dreadful silence followed my cheerful greeting. I was not invited to sit down and after some painful moments I just offered my love-gift and said farewell. I can assure you that I did not feel very victorious when I walked back to my home. I cried bitter tears. Yet I had obeyed God's command and I made a point of praying God's blessing over their lives, even after they had left our town. The relationship with them was never restored, but I can honestly say that there has not remained any bitterness in my heart towards them. It was a very difficult but valuable experience in my own spiritual life, and I can encourage you to give it a try as well.

If you have trouble with people in the church who are

criticising you, invite them for dinner! If somebody is gossiping about you, bring her a home-made cake, or a bunch of flowers. Do something totally unusual, something nice and revolutionary—that is what the Lord calls us to do. It is easy to say that we love our enemies. With the word 'enemy' we think mainly about war, about soldiers with guns, but those are often far away from us and to love them is not so difficult.

But the Lord rather means that neighbour who talks badly about us, or that couple who turned against us and is hindering us on all fronts! He means that man who worked your husband out of the evangelism committee! Those are the enemies who keep us awake at night. Don't take revenge, but love them, give to them and lend to them without hope of a response. Is that devout and cheap talk? No, this is very practical but very difficult. It's love that costs us something. It is a matter of doing, of taking a decision that runs counter to all human feelings. If you are doing it, check your motivation. Don't do it in order to gain people's favour or to bribe them, which would only result in you becoming even more disappointed and bitter! Do it without expecting anything in return (Luke 6:35). Why should we then do it? Is this not totally crazy? Humanly speaking yes, but not from God's point of view. 'Then...you will be sons of the Most High, because he is kind to the ungrateful and wicked' (Luke 6:35). I think that this is the only motivation for acting this way. Only God, his character, his love and his command can bring us this far.

Give it a try! God will bless you and your reward will be in heaven.

7. *Be strong.* Do you ever watch political debates? Sometimes you can hardly believe the way they treat one another. I have often thought that you need an elephant skin in order to survive in the political world. Politicians

work hard. We know that lots of them honestly try to do everything possible to lead the country out of a jungle of problems, cutbacks, and opposing interests. Of course they earn a good salary for their hard work. However, they have to put up with a lot of criticism. The opposition attacks everything they undertake and even their character, devotion and integrity is continually publicly questioned. Do you think politicians sometimes cry into their pillows because of all the criticism? Maybe, but in general they make a very strong impression, and many of them keep going for years. They seem to be convinced of their ideology and their goal. Even if their foundations seem to shake, they press on.

We could learn something from this mentality. Of course, we cannot continue on our road of stubbornness, hard-headedness, pride, and insensitivity. James says that the wisdom from above is friendly and submissive. However, I still think that most of us, myself included, should become a little bit more firm emotionally.

David ends his thirty-first Psalm, in which he wrestles with the criticism of others, with the words: 'Be strong and take heart, all you who hope in the Lord.' This is a call, an encouragement, a challenge: be strong!

In the letter to the Hebrews we are encouraged to fix our eyes on Jesus, who endured strong opposition from sinful men, so that we will not grow weary and lose heart (Hebrews 12:2,3). You can get so tired from all the criticism. You can get so fed up with being continually misunderstood, that you indeed lose your fire and zeal. Your soul grows tired and weary. When I was a child and my parents were middle-aged, there was often enormous pressure on them. We had a clothes shop, and my parents worked in the shop all day long, being busy serving people. In the evenings they had yet more responsibilities. They led Bible study groups, prayer meetings and youth groups. On Sundays my father preached in different churches while my mother played the organ and after church we rushed off to Sunday school. There were also the usual family problems and church problems. My father often heaved a sigh at the table and said: 'I wish I had become a wood-cutter! It must be wonderful to spend the whole day alone in the woods with only the trees, the birds and God as company!'

Do you know this feeling? However, the Bible does not give us grounds to give in to our 'wood-cutter syndrome'. On the contrary: 'Therefore, strengthen your feeble arms and weak knees! Make level paths for your feet, so that the lame may not be disabled, but rather healed' (Hebrews 12:12,13).

When criticism has hurt us, we need healing. This healing can necessitate withdrawing for a little while into the woods to get our breath back, but in the long run we need something else: strengthen your feeble arms and weak knees, let the ankles that have been kicked start going again, otherwise the dents remain there and they will end up being stiff and lame. Training and physiotherapy are necessary! Get up out of your corner of self-pity and bitterness. Put your hopes upon the Lord and be strong. God has given us a spirit of power (2 Timothy 1:7) and he encourages us to be strong in his grace (2 Timothy 2:1). He does not say this from his ivory tower, not knowing what he is talking about. He has been tempted in all these things just like us, he took all the criticism and betrayal to the last, but he did not give up. He is offering us his grace. That grace was sufficient for Paul in this same battle with criticism and misunderstanding. That is his side of the business. Our side is to get up and to become strong and courageous.

'Be strong and take heart, all you who hope in the Lord' (Psalm 31:24).

Conclusion: God Is Great

In this book, I have tried to give you a taste of the possibilities that God opens up for us.

It is true that things will not always go smoothly. It is also true that we have to start giving our active co-operation in the areas where God wants to work in and through our lives. Peter admonishes us to be all the more eager to make our calling sure (2 Peter 1:10). He means confirming our calling, not bringing it about. The initiative of our calling lies with God. He has chosen us before the foundation of the world. He has done everything to pay the price for our reconciliation. He took us out of darkness and brought us into the kingdom of his beloved Son. He thought of it all and brought it about and in his grace offered it to us. What he is asking from us is to accept it thankfully and then to give our fervent co-operation in what he has prepared for us (Ephesians 2:10). In the preceding chapters we have seen the ways in which we can work with that in everyday life.

In all of this it is of the utmost importance never to lose sight of God and his beautiful characteristics. If we are getting actively engaged in his work, there is a great danger of going under by trying to become better and more spiritual while on the other side we are getting snowed under by our Christian activities. This is a danger for everyone who wants to serve the Lord, on the mission field as well as at home. That's why it is of the utmost importance that we keep our biblical priorities straight.

God's grace

Grace is a beautiful word that is used time and time again to show us how God thinks and acts. Grace is an unmerited gift which God offers to us. Grace is a word laden with love, mercy, and compassion. Almost all Paul's letters begin with the words: 'Grace and peace to you from God our Father and the Lord Jesus Christ'. Even though God is so holy, just and perfect, he does not come to us with his demands. He comes to us with grace! Paul also says farewell in most of his letters with the words 'Grace be with you'. It is grace at the beginning and grace at the end. In Ephesians 2 Paul says: 'For it is by grace you have been saved' (verse 8). He also speaks about the grace of our Lord which was poured out on him abundantly (1 Timothy 1:14). 'By the grace of God I am what I am' (1 Corinthians 15:10). This is so wonderful!

It is true that God wants us to be active workers for him, but the keyword is grace, with which everything started, develops and ends. It is of the utmost importance that we make this truth our own. Just like the people of Galatia we run the danger of starting with grace, but halfway down the track, resorting to our own works and our own efforts to serve God. About Jesus it is written that in his youth he grew in grace with God and men (Luke 2:52). Grace was there, rich and abundant, and still the Lord Jesus grew in that grace. In that same way we can give a free hand to grace in our life in order to grow in it. Peter ended his second letter with the encouragement: 'But grow in the grace and knowledge of our Lord and Saviour Jesus Christ.'

The author of the letter to the Hebrews describes God's throne as a throne of grace. He encourages us fervently to approach the throne with confidence, so that we may receive mercy and find grace to help us in our time of need. Hold on to this, never let it go! It is the most precious thing we have received in Christ. Grace! Grace to live for him, grace to, if necessary, suffer for him (Philippians 1:29, 1 Peter 2:20) and grace to die. Difficulties, sorrows, weariness and bitterness are all things through which we can miss the grace of God (Hebrews 12:1–17). Don't let that happen! Hold on to that grace, become firm in that grace and grow in it. Watch out lest life only becomes a race against yourself. God's grace is like the warm summer sun, wonderful, abundant and beneficial. It sends the cold chills in our life on the run! God's grace is like a hot bath, relaxing and restoring. It dispels the weariness of our own attempts and failures. God's grace is enough, more than enough. It is present in a wonderful way to take a hold of us and to equip us and to show everyone how great the richness of his grace is. God's grace is wonderful! God is wonderful!

God's love

God's love is closely linked to his grace. It is because of his great love with which he loved us that we are saved by his grace! (Ephesians 2:4,5). The Bible even goes further. God does not only have a great love for us, God is love (1 John 4:16). His whole being is love. If we could only be more convinced about this, then many things that hinder us would often find their right place. It is of the utmost importance to allow this fact to penetrate through and through; that this love is not there because we loved God, but because he loved us and to prove this he sent his Son as a reconciliation for our sin (1 John

4:10). Do you see that the initiative of everything lies in him and in his love? That's why nothing can separate us from his love. It does not depend on the circumstances. It does not depend on other people. It does not depend on us.

'No, in all these things we are more than conquerors through him who loved us. For I am convinced that neither death nor life, neither angels nor demons, neither the present nor the future, nor any powers, neither height nor depth, nor anything else in all creation, will be able to separate us from the love of God that is in Christ Jesus our Lord' (Romans 8:37–39). God's love is great! God is great!

God is merciful

The Lord is compassionate and gracious! (Psalm 103:8). All these wonderful attitudes of God overlap and are linked to one another. God's mercy stretches from generation to generation (Luke 1:50). This is fantastic! God was merciful to our forefathers, he was merciful to our father and mother. He is merciful to us and he will be merciful to our children. The fact that God offers us knowledge of salvation through the forgiveness of our sins is because of the tender mercy of our God (Luke 1:77,78). He is also called the Father of compassion (2 Corinthians 1:3) and in his great mercy he has given us new birth (1 Peter 1:3). Do you see that the same aspect is underlined? The initiative of all these things is not in us, but in God. He wants mercy, peace and love to be ours in abundance (Jude 2). God's mercy is great! God is great!

God's comfort

God is the Father of compassion and the God of all comfort who comforts us in all our troubles (2 Corinthians 1:4). God's mercy is closely linked to his comfort. In the Old Testament God says to his people: 'I, even I, am he who comforts you' (Isaiah 51:12) and 'As a mother comforts her child, so will I comfort you' (Isaiah 66:13). 'Comfort, comfort my people, says your God' (Isaiah 40:1).

All three persons of the Godhead are described as comforters; 'God our Father, who loved us and by his grace gave us eternal encouragement' (2 Thessalonians 2:16). The Lord Jesus is described in Luke 2:25 as the comforter of Israel, and the Holy Spirit is called the Comforter by the Lord Jesus, especially given to us to comfort us in a life that is not always easy.

Do you get a picture of God's character? He is full of grace, love, mercy and comfort. Read the Bible, feed yourself on these truths. We need to learn to know God as he presents himself to us. God's comfort is great! God is great!

God is great! His strength, power and majesty are great! His character of love, grace, mercy and comfort is great! He is offering all this to us. If we accept it with gratitude from his hand, then our lives become a feast.

NOT ONLY FOR OURSELVES

The biblical message goes further. God's love does not stop with us, his children. God's love is much greater, embracing a lot more. God loved us before we became his children! He loved us while we were still sinners. And now, now that we are his children, this is not the end of his love. God loves the world! God loves the millions of people who walk the streets of the big cities. He knows each one of them personally. His grace is available to our neighbours who want to have nothing to do with our God. His mercy reaches to a world that doesn't know mercy, and in which people are driven on and become weary like sheep without a shepherd. That's why the Lord Jesus cries out with indignation to the religious people of his time: 'But go and learn what this means: "I desire mercy, not sacrifice" ' (Matthew 9:13). God's comfort is great. But his comfort does not stop at our tears. God's comfort wants to reach out to all those people who have lost everything, all those people who lead a hopeless existence in the refugee camps of northern Pakistan, of Thailand, of Sudan and Lebanon.

It is wonderful, refreshing and often necessary to take new courage out of God's never-drying wells. However, God wants to go further. He wants to put those wells of love, grace and comfort in our own hearts in order to exhibit his characteristics in this world.

If he loves us and gave his life for us, then he wants our love in return, by going into this world and imparting this love through our hands, through our eyes and through our voice, to people who don't believe in love any more, and to children who have never experienced love.

John, the apostle who more than anybody else referred to this love, says: 'Dear children, let us not love with words or tongue but with actions and in truth' (1 John 3:18), 'Whoever does not love does not know God, because God is love' (1 John 4:8).

Grace, comfort and mercy have the same common goal. God gives them to us in order to refresh us and to strengthen us. The goal is not for our benefit only. God comforts us, so that we can comfort those with the comfort we ourselves have received (2 Corinthians 1:4).

The whole world

How do you get to that? By first receiving it abundantly from God himself. Live with God, dedicate your life to him, take that decision and be serious in spending daily time with God. Give God the opportunity to do a deep, healing work in your soul with all its complexities and problems, through his grace. But don't concentrate only upon yourself! Look to the people around you. Talk to the woman whose husband just ran off. Show some love to that mother who just lost her child. Make contacts, show love and friendliness. A smile is often sufficient to open a door for friendship.

But don't let your interests be limited to your street, your school, your church. The world is so much bigger! Take every opportunity to broaden your knowledge of that world. God loves the world. There are millions of people who have never heard the name of Jesus, who live without love, without hope and without comfort. Go and visit mission meetings, read magazines about mission work and relief work. Follow programmes about countries and their needs on television. It doesn't matter which political party made the programme. They all depict the tragedy of a world without God. Buy a world map. Find out where a certain country is located, learn your geography, better late than never! We are dealing with God's world, the world he loves and for which he gave and sent his Son. In John 20:21 Jesus gives us the command: 'As the Father has sent me, I am sending you.' He sends us the same way, filled with the same characteristics. Full of love, comfort, mercy and grace he sends us into this world. He sends us while he is still developing and unfolding these characteristics in our own lives.

A FEAST

God is great. If we get to know him and when his
character is developing in us, then life becomes a feast.
But he never wanted to limit this feast to only a few. God
is preparing a great feast. The poor, the needy, the
blind, the lame and the beggars of this world are part of
God's chosen guests. In his impartial love and mercy,
God wants to use you and me to gather the guests for this
feast. If we obey God in this and in dependence upon
him start working, then life will become a feast, a feast in
which we are allowed to be God's co-workers. Co-
workers who are not yet perfect, but who are being
polished in the process.